Values-Based Business Design

Values-Based Business Design

MODERN PRODUCT DEVELOPMENT FOR HIGH-GROWTH COMPANIES

Lasean Smith

VALUES-BASED BUSINESS DESIGN

Modern Product Development
for High-Growth Companies

ISBN 978-1-62301-001-0 Paperback
978-1-62301-002-7 Ebook

TO LORRAINE:

Thanks for giving me the space to think

(and for still loving books).

CONTENTS

INTRODUCTION

THIS BOOK WAS WRITTEN TO PROVIDE A SET OF TOOLS AND insights to improve your customer relationships. I hope it helps you build something amazing.

In my current role at a large software company, I manage business design for commercial and consumer products. My focus is customer retention and monetization, or answering the following question: How do you get people to continually give you time and money in exchange for the value you're providing them? This question is an interesting distillation of business because at the most basic level, that's all business is—offering value in a way that helps people reach their aspirations or solve their problems. In exchange, they give you—you hope—their time and/or money.

My journey to working in product strategy was built on several other paths that coalesced into this one. Growing up, my parents focused on continuing their education as a way to empower themselves and increase their economic opportunities. They each went back to school at various points, and for a good portion of that time, my dad was in the military. We moved several times, allowing me to see firsthand a wide landscape of lifestyles and values, and the variety of environments and cultures that people call home. That experience anchored my view of the world.

As a kid, I had a great family support and structure, but when I later tried to break into business, I didn't know anyone in that world. My grandmother was the closest person to me who resembled an entrepreneur. She sold her wares, on a very small scale, to the neighborhood. Other than her as a reference point, I didn't know anyone in business. I didn't even know anyone who worked in an office.

Entrepreneurship fascinated me. I tried my best to play in that world and, more importantly, to learn all I could about it. I made many mistakes along the way, but my commitment to figuring out what it takes to be an entrepreneur was part of my journey very early on.

When I was nine years old, my mom went with one of her friends on an errand to a warehouse store. I had no idea what was inside that big building, but I was curious and couldn't resist asking to go look. My mom left the car running while I tagged along with her friend and went inside, imagining all kinds of possibilities as to what the warehouse might hold.

Once inside, my eyes fell on racks and shelves of candy as far as I could see. This was the first time I had ever seen so many items in bulk. My mom's friend went to pick up a box they had ready for her. It turned out that she was a reseller, and this was where she came to buy bulk snacks, chips, and candy.

While she was wrapping up her transaction, I strolled over to a shelf containing an open box of candy. It happened to be boxes of Chick-O-Sticks, a sweet and crunchy brown-sugar candy. It was mind-boggling how many there were in that box. My nine-year-old brain asked for the price and tried to do the math. I realized the candy here was much cheaper than at the grocery store.

My mind had been opened to a different world, one where I calculated the cost margins and found there was an opportunity to buy this candy and sell it to other people for a profit. I came back a week later and bought twenty dollars' worth of product for resale. I took the candy back to my neighborhood playground and charged the retail price.

Because kids couldn't normally go to the store by themselves at that age, this gave them a convenient opportunity to purchase candy. And they did: I sold all of it within forty-eight hours.

When it was gone, I knew I had something to work with. Over time, I started finding other sources to obtain my products. I wasn't licensed to use the wholesaler account, after all, and needed my business to become legit.

Through buying and selling, I gained insight into what people wanted. I noticed that boys wanted cigarette-shaped chewing gum sticks, while girls preferred candy rings—lollipops that resembled oversize wedding rings. Those items were more expensive to procure, so my profit margins were low. I told the kids they could get either of those items if they bought some other type of candy as well. That's how I stumbled into bundling.

Bundling became a way for me to move the inventory that wasn't working, and kids were still happy because it wasn't like the other products were something they didn't want—these goods just weren't at the top of their list. The desire for those top-shelf items was so strong that the kids would do seemingly irrational things. Observing them, I learned about my customers' aspirations. For the girls, the ring candy was a symbol of social status just as a diamond ring is for a woman. It signified that they had attention from the boys. Of course, this was actually well-documented marketing exercise that the diamond industry was doing to condition girls to their product early in life.

I started to see several implied values in the way those kids behaved, which I didn't fully understand as impactful or profound at the time. But in hindsight, the girls who bought the ring candy are really no different than any other consumer. If you sell within the context of the customers' values, they will keep buying from you.

This concept of "selling in context" is the focus of this book. To pull it off, you have to fundamentally understand both your customers' values and the real value your product provides within the context of those values. It's an important distinction to separate value from values.

A customer's values are the principles that drive and motivate him or her and guide his or her decisions. His or her values help him or her figure out who he or she is going to be. These very basic values can be anything from language to humor, family, and ambition. A person's values shape who he or she is at his or her core.

When we discuss the word *value*, we're usually talking about value propositions or the value of a product. Values and value are connected, but the distinction is worth underscoring, and it begins with finding authentic ways of uncovering the customers' values, then determining the value of the product in that context.

If you want to know who or what a person stands for, ask him or her for a half dozen key words that describe him-/herself: *approachable*, *curious*, *intelligence*, *joyfulness*, *predictability*, and *timeliness*, for example, might represent someone's list. Which of those values represents who he or she really is? It forces him or her to think about not just his or her beliefs but also about his or her behaviors in the context of those beliefs.

Where customers see the world acknowledging and advancing those values, they'll have a strong affinity for those relationships and types of products. Now, people may not always exhibit the behaviors associated with these cherished values. I've heard people say, "I value predictability, but I'm really disorganized." That statement is very revealing of a place in which you can provide value.

There's a definition of happiness that says, "Happiness is your perceived reality of the world minus your expectations of it." With regard to the statement above, "I value predictability, but I'm really disorganized," there is a disconnect between one's expectations of predictability and one's reality of disorganization, and that leads to unhappiness. Anything that bridges the two will be seen as welcome and will provide a lot of value.

When people say that opposites attract, what they are often acknowledging is that there are gaps between our aspirations and our realities, and when a person is able to help fill that gap, that relationship provides value. So if I value predictability but am really disorganized, but you are able to bring organization into my life, that value you offer may well manifest itself as attraction.

I didn't learn all of this selling candy on a playground when I was nine, but that's indeed where it started. And at a certain point, I had earned enough to buy a computer. I begged my mother to let me get the TRS-80 MC-10 (this was back in the 1980s, when computers could have a terribly obscure name). It was on sale for $59 and it hooked up directly to the television set.

My TRS-80 MC-10 was by no means a high-powered computer—my phone has far more computational power—but it unlocked for me the world of computing and set me on a path of technology in which I could take my observations and insights and apply them to an industry that would become a veritable rocket ship over the course of the 1980s and 1990s.

I didn't do an analysis to decide I wanted to be in technology, nor build any software to figure out if I was good at it. I just picked what was interesting to me, which turned out to be a megatrend on a macro level.

One morning, my mom saw me on the computer and commented on how early I had woken up to work. She immediately realized her mistake. I had been sitting in the chair the entire night. On one level, I believe she wanted me to find my own thing in life, but on another level, she realized she couldn't have a kid playing on his computer twenty hours a day. Nevertheless, that first computer paved the way for a better computer, as I was saving all my money from candy sales.

When I was about thirteen, I took a city bus to an IBM store, which sold desktop computers. Young boys in Michael Jordan jerseys and acid-washed jeans were not IBM's target demographic. Nevertheless, the salesman was very nice and walked me through the cost, options, and add-ons. The computer I wanted was going to cost about $3,000 plus shipping. Meanwhile, my parents had no idea what I was up to.

About a month after I paid for it, I received a message on the answering machine about delivery, addressing me as "Mr.

Smith." Ha! I deleted it. When the computer arrived, it was fantastic. A wave of euphoria rushed over me as I opened the box. I got rid of the packaging and sold my old computer at a pawn shop—there was no Craigslist back then. I set up the new machine, and it was like magic.

That day of discovering bulk candy at the warehouse store and all of the selling that I'd done since had led to this device. And now that I owned one, it showed me the empowerment that technology can provide. Ever since then, I've been hooked.

I used to think the technology industry was a special little club for people who had the discipline to consistently sit in front of their computer for twenty hours at a time. Great technologists use that time to deeply understand customers and their environment. If you're really good at building software that millions of people connect with, you most likely built a set of frameworks and a process to understand how to get a product to resonate with someone's values. Such skills are useful not just in the realm of technology but also for anyone creating a product or service. And it's not a special club. It's just an approach to product development that anyone can take advantage of.

This book is for people inside and outside the technology industry. It's for the solopreneur, the one-person entrepreneur trying to create a product that grows quickly. It's for the C-level executives' and product managers' long-term company planning. It's for the small businesses that may be time- or resource constrained. Even large, resource-rich companies that have been established for years can apply these tools and find success in existing or future products. Anyone who desires to build a global, high-growth product will benefit.

I've spent the majority of my professional career focused on taking things that don't exist and growing them to a global scale very quickly. This book shares some of the actionable steps to do that in a more predictable manner.

I've spoken with and mentored a number of entrepreneurs—owners of traditional small businesses, as well as owners of start-ups trying to find a rapid accelerator to grow quickly. The excuse I often hear is that if they had more funding, they could make it work. They think a lack of resources excludes them from success and that if they could get those resources, they could build a prototype, buy some advertising, do media buys, find a media partner, or hire a full-time sales team.

The reality is, those things are useful when applied appropriately but aren't key indicators as to whether a company, small or large, will succeed in launching and sustaining a high-growth product.

The grass isn't always greener on the other side; it's just different grass. When I talk to people in different industries or who have different business models, they always seem to think another option would be better for them. The company that has an advertising-based model believes if they only had subscriptions, all their problems would be solved. The consumer product manager thinks that if he only had commercial- or enterprise-type business models where he had fewer people to take money from, all his problems would be solved. Then, they start looking at each other. Big companies that aren't innovating buy little companies to help fix what they're lacking. Little companies, in turn, think they don't have the ability to buy television or radio ads or spend money on digital marketing campaigns in any way comparable to the big companies.

It often turns out that the traditional marketing approach is what's turning off customers. The good news is that the old way of doing things isn't the long-term solution. Armed with the information within these pages, a small company with the right perspective can have a legitimate shot even without access to a lot of capital, while a large company can move more quickly by breaking free from much of its perceived bureaucracy to spend its money more wisely. Both can have success with high-growth products if they embrace some of these concepts.

What I hear from executives at large companies is that they need to innovate, but typically, the most innovative technologies don't actually win. The company that creates the technology first is not always the company that succeeds with it. Technological innovation isn't bad, of course, but nobody should think that it is necessary to develop a winning strategy.

There are multiple types of intellectual property protection in the United States. For instance, copyright is used primarily to protect creative works, such as a painting, song lyrics, or a novel. Patents protect inventions or processes. Trademarks protect a brand name or a logo. Trade secrets can also be protected, as long as the company doesn't share them. Coca-Cola, for example, never patented its recipe because the patent protection would have eventually expired. Instead, it decided to keep the formula a trade secret, and because it never shared the recipe publicly, it would have legal recourse if the recipe was ever stolen. In many of the fastest-growing industries, there is no protection for the intellectual property (IP) being created.

If someone wants to launch a new pharmaceutical company, a power plant, or any business that's relatively capital intensive, there are reasons why IP protection still makes sense. In many other cases, the way that companies interact with customers has changed to the point where, if they have a software product, for example, and they find a more interesting way in the user interface to help solve someone's problem more quickly, there's very little they can do to use IP protection to make sure their competitor doesn't copy it.

This, however, actually turns out to be a good thing because it forces the industry to feed off one another, and the best ideas win out. It moves the evolution of that product category much more rapidly, as evidenced in everything from web browsers to mobile apps. Think about the way your cable box used to look, and compare that with an Amazon Fire Stick, Apple TV, or Roku, and all of these products have moved very quickly because everyone's trying to win the customer relationship.

Technological innovation is not the winning strategy for most products. Many times, if a company realizes it is not going to win through technical innovation, it decides to be a great marketer. This strategy involves incorporating the leading innovators' fantastic features, benefits, and other attributes. The goal is to take what someone else has created and repackage it with a better marketing campaign.

That strategy, too, involves risk. Companies have been successfully buying their way into customers' lives for years. But in this age of information, trust has eroded in an era of transparency and as customers have grown more sophisticated and, resultantly, more cynical. This is even more pronounced among millennials and younger customer segments, who make use of the Internet and share information through social media, among other means. Consequently, the cynicism is extremely high in terms of whether an advertisement is telling the truth.

There was a time, fifteen to twenty years ago, when a company could create an ab cruncher and claim, "Will give you a six-pack in six weeks, so call now!" It would even entice consumers to buy the ab cruncher by throwing in bonus items. Those bonus items are, of course, a ploy to get the consumer to react in the moment. The bonus items, like the ab cruncher itself, are tied directly to the consumer's values, which, in this case, might be the most bang for his or her buck.

What people value and how they actually behave are the difference between attitudinal and behavioral realities. If someone says, "I really want the six-pack, but I know I'm not exercising or eating right." What he or she is saying is, "I want this other thing but not at the expense of these other values that I, in fact, have deemed more important." What this person deems as more important is convenience. That value, convenience, is exactly what the ab cruncher machine is promising.

Similar selling strategies are still seen on networks, such as QVC, for instance, but consumers are able to research items on sites, such as Amazon, before purchasing. They type in "ab cruncher," and they see the same one that they saw on the TV infomercial. They can now see the one-star aggregate review of the product. They can now read reviews from people who aren't even in their social circle: "Oh, way smaller than it looked on the commercial," "No good," "I stored it and the edges started to curve a weird way." They read this, and suddenly, all of that marketing momentum has been deflated. They lose interest, close the tab, and they're off doing something else.

The ability to buy more media, to be louder than that crowd-sourced voice on the Internet, hits the tipping point where it's not economically feasible for marketers to buy their way out of products that aren't authentic. The Internet and social media are connected, and the way people are getting introduced to new products is through their social circles. If companies want a product to show up authentically in conversations, executives need to find out whom they can build connections with.

Those connections then introduce the product to that particular social circle instead of treating consumers as a homogeneous, disconnected group that can be reached through the lowest common denominator method of broadcast media. This approach isn't as powerful anymore because consumers are more informed and they're talking to one another.

You can't bet on technical innovation to win. You can't guarantee the success of a marketing campaign nor can you buy your way to high-growth sales. The products and companies that develop the best relationships with their customers are the ones that win. Those have to be authentic relationships. Money can't buy friendship, as The Beatles explained in the lyrics of "Can't Buy Me Love."

There is something about a great relationship that makes you feel as if that other entity is there for you even when you don't give them what they might want or need in the moment. There is enough trust built up that you know if you need them, they will be there for you, doing what they're good at doing.

Brands have not embraced that, primarily because it seemed like something that wouldn't scale very well: it's very expensive and it's hard to make it a clear process. If you have a set of brand managers or product managers, and you let them build direct one-to-one relationships and one of them quits, there's fear that one manager could take those relationships to a competitor.

These authentic relationships are great, to be certain, but the company doesn't own them. If you have more authentic relationships, you will be more competitive. Companies haven't had a repeatable framework or process on how they can implement that, so they have largely avoided it. This book is going to give people the tools so that can change.

There are three key areas that this book will address:

- First, the way we're doing traditional business and product design is wrong. This is not just because we're spending money inefficiently, but also because we're building the wrong type of relationships with our customers. It's important to better understand what's gone wrong before figuring out how to solve it.

- Second, we will look at the history of why this environment exists at all. It's important to better understand the dynamics we face, whether at large companies or in small start-ups, to understand why this inertia in the wrong direction has been perpetuated for so long.

- Finally, I want you, the reader, to put this into action. You can't just talk theory and get results. You have to figure out ways to make it real—not just real in the context of some of the examples that the book will walk through, but to make sure you have a framework such that they can be applied in a very actionable manner.

There is a seven-step structured approach that the latter part of the book will use to walk you through any existing or new product that you're looking to put on a high-growth trajectory.

PART I

BUSINESS DESIGN YESTERDAY AND TODAY

CHAPTER 1

THE PROBLEM

TRADITIONAL BUSINESS DESIGN, MEANING THE SET OF ACTIVITIES that defines how a company will stay in business at every juncture from launch to growth to customer loyalty, requires both qualitative and quantitative research, product feature iteration, business model experimentation, exploration of different ways to structure teams in the organization, partnerships, intellectual property strategy, and so on. Doing all of this well can be hard, and it is part of the reason so many of today's companies are building products that simply aren't that great.

Smart companies have developed techniques to make up for these deficiencies. One such technique is marketing. So, if the product isn't amazing, a company may try to spend its way out of these deficiencies. And there was a time when that was a viable solution.

As we've come to discover, however, that strategy doesn't work in today's connected world. We live in the context of the Internet and the information age. What traditional business design does not systematically take into account is that customers have much better buying information at their fingertips. As a result, companies can't solely advertise or market their way to sustain product growth. Instead, they need to build a better product, and to do that, they need a better relationship with the customer.

Case in point, back in the 1990s when I was selling candy and trying to buy that first computer, one of the things kids did was visit retail stores and actually buy CDs. True story. And back then, there were many stores to choose from. There was Tower Records, of course, and Sam Goody and The Wherehouse, and there were local mom-and-pop stores. Then big-box stores started popping up.

Technically, these stores had been around for years. The Circuit Citys and the Best Buys, started in the 1960s and 1970s, focused on selling radios or other types of electronics equipment. Those brands exploded in the late 1980s and 1990s, and they became places where you could buy all sorts of products—including music. There were also places like Blockbuster where you could rent a VHS, maybe even a DVD. There was a whole set of players in this industry, from the marketing and demand generation on radio and music videos, to the distribution of their products, to the retailing of these products, where these businesses had extreme inefficiencies. And they got away with it because the customer didn't have the information to know whether the product was any good.

During that period, music CDs were pretty expensive. Adjusted for inflation in today's dollars, they're even more expensive, but even in absolute dollars back then, a CD cost around $18. The concept of paying $18 for an album would seem silly in today's world, but on Tuesdays, these companies would release new music to great fanfare. These boxes of plastic discs would show up on a Friday, Saturday, or Sunday. Then, retailers would unpack them, and on Tuesday morning, when they opened their doors, the latest NSYNC album would be on the store shelves. People were ready to buy them.

The way a customer promise worked at that time involved the customer hearing a song on the radio, watching a music video on the TV, and hearing the buzz at school about it. Based on that fairly limited information, having heard but one or two songs, which represented maybe 10 percent or perhaps 20 percent of the product, they would still commit to buying that relatively high-priced CD.

Customers were fine with that for a little while. The cost seemed justified. It was fairly expensive, even though the prices were falling, to create this content. Companies had to pay the record producer, the songwriter, the musicians, the artist, even the graphic designer or photographer responsible for the cover art, as well as the rest of their overhead, including all of the promotions, which was sometimes an even bigger expense.

While there may have been many CDs to choose from, if people had a certain affinity for a specific genre, there may have been only a half dozen releases that day. They could quickly look through those, make their decision, and off they go. People bought a lot of CDs. As a result, the record labels, retailers, and promotional channels—such as radio and cable TV—were all under pressure to grow. The goal was to capture as much of the customers' disposable income as possible.

Big-box companies were, for the most part, public companies under constant pressure to grow. One of the most common growth strategies was to open new stores wherever large neighborhoods of new houses were being built. The housing boom was starting to take off at this time, leading stores to open in more suburban areas.

The record labels were also looking to grow, or at least increase their profits. They began aggressively looking for ways to save and reduce costs. One way to save costs was to make more content with lower quality. So the labels increased the number of CD releases every Tuesday. They gave the record producers and artists fewer resources and less money and less time to produce them. But they kept charging the same price to customers.

The retailers realized what the labels were doing and decided they could get more customers in the store by discounting the CDs. Once the customer was in the store, the retailer would try to sell them an appliance or stereo. Remember, these big-box stores were largely located in suburban areas where people were trying to furnish newly built homes. So rather than try to sell CDs for $18, they started selling them for as low as $10.

There was no compulsory law that forced these retailers to sell the music at a certain price, so sometimes they would even sell it at or under cost. That became the business model for these big-box players. They were using music to sell something else. The concept of selling a loss leader wasn't new—hey, I was even doing it on the playground with my candy. However, the music industry allowed this to evolve into full-on customer exploitation.

The executives of the companies who used this model believed it would just keep going in perpetuity. They had found their growth engine. There were still albums made by quality artists who produced great music during this period, but the amount of junk that came out at the same time started to erode customers' faith.

Retailers began to lose their customers' trust because there was no curation happening with the music they sold. They simply accepted whatever music the record labels sent them regardless of the quality. And much of that music was very low quality, with albums featuring perhaps one hit single and seven or eight tracks that served essentially as filler. Nevertheless, companies didn't start getting called out until the beginning of the Internet age.

Record labels and retailers were extremely short-sighted. They highly underestimated the impact and the transformation that would be delivered by the Internet. Consumers were able to procure better information. They were, at last, able to see inside the package of the product they had been previously purchasing blindly.

Rather than going to Circuit City and putting on headphones at a retail kiosk, where they could sample the four featured albums, consumers could now listen to literally thousands of songs on demand. Digital publishing also took off at this time through blogs and unpaid reviews. These reviews weren't from magazines that relied on advertising money from the record labels to stay in business, and because of this, they became more and more authentic. Now consumers could look up this information and know if an album was any good before they made the purchase.

Marketers tried to keep up, but many of them permanently lost the trust of their customers. It's an important definition in the context of this book as I talk about how to understand trust. There is a definition that I've shortened and abbreviated from multiple sources to be very actionable: trust is our ability to predict future behavior.

If someone doesn't trust an individual or a brand, it's highly unlikely that a value exchange happens. I've talked about the core of what a product is trying to do, which is to exchange time and money. If I don't trust your brand or your product, I'm not giving you either of those. A personal relationship is a good example of why trust is so meaningful.

People often use the word *trust* as if it's a positive thing that can be built up or lost but stays inherently positive. Trust is neither positive nor negative; it is simply the ability to predict future behavior. If someone is in a relationship and his or her partner cheats on him or her, what he or she might say is, "I don't trust you anymore." What he or she is really saying is, "I have a set of expectations that guide me. I use these expectations and rules to figure out how you should show up in my life. Because you've cheated, I can no longer predict that you will follow my rules. As a result of that, it's really hard for me to maintain this relationship with you."

There are public examples that can be found with celebrities. Tiger Woods, for example, created a very family-centric persona during his early years on the national stage. And his brand, despite the occasional foul word after a stray tee shot, was squeaky clean. He made an implicit promise to show excellence both on and off the greens as a man of family values. Then, scandals were revealed in his personal life, and everyone was shocked because they didn't believe he was such a different person than his professional persona. The result? The public no longer trusted him; he lost endorsements, and the damage is still felt to this day.

Now, compare that to someone like George Clooney, who for years built a persona on his bachelorhood. He never made any implicit promises like Woods did, and as a result, there were no tabloid articles whenever he would break up with a girlfriend and move on to the next one.

People may not embrace or even agree with that lifestyle, but there was no cause for outrage when one of his relationships ended. People give that behavior a pass because they feel they understand how George Clooney will behave in the future. When he finally did marry, it may have come as a shock to many who believed he would stay single his whole life, but it was mostly seen in a positive light, depicting an evolution rather than, as in Woods's case, a fraud.

Many times for brands, because of the nature of the short cycles of marketing campaigns and the short-term growth based on quarterly reports in which CEOs are managing businesses, companies behave as if their customers have the memory of goldfish. And when they finally get called out on this behavior, they promise they will do better. The partner who has cheated is also asking for trust, promising that this time it's going to be different. However, the trust has been lost at that point.

A company might have a new go-to market strategy that it's launching that is going to really take its latest product to new heights, but the customer—more elephant than goldfish—still remembers vividly what that company did to him or her last time around. This is basic, but companies have continued to neglect this.

Let's get back to the impact of the story of the big-box retailers that were selling music in the 1990s. Unsurprisingly, it all started to fall apart. You can point to Napster and similar services that helped speed up this decline. But the truth is, the music industry didn't implode because of Napster or digital piracy; those were just accelerants, gasoline on the fire. The reason it was smoldering in the first place was because these businesses were exploiting their customers. It's a different feeling when someone robs you as opposed to another criminal. I'm not suggesting in any way that these companies were doing something illegal. However, it is inauthentic for the labels and retailers to believe that they could exploit their customers but that no one was allowed to exploit them in return. Customers, once empowered, ended a toxic relationship with the exploitative record label-retailer complex.

The impact of that divorce has been profound. Number one, the record labels didn't try to build authentic relationships. There were fan clubs that certain artists had, but the only real data that was collected were retail data at the point of sale. There is something that still exists today called Nielsen Music Sales Measurement (formerly SoundScan). When the UPC code, the unique bar code on the back of the product, is scanned, Nielsen is able to track it. This was a service optimized for brick-and-mortar music retailing. Sometimes CDs didn't have bar codes, so a mom-and-pop retailer might write the sales information in a ledger.

Through various data collections—whether it was scanning a bar code into an electronic system or sending a ledger back to someone who would then reconcile it—these reports would come out with statistics about how many copies of this NSYNC album were sold and where. That was useful data because artists could interpret it and respond accordingly. For instance, they could plan concert tours based on their record sales in certain cities.

But in that system there is no conversation going on with the customer. Even the retailers did a horrible job with building real customer relationships. With myriad opportunities to gather information to improve customer relations, the retailers did nothing. For the most part, US retailers kept only the zip codes of their customers, and that was only if a credit card was used as payment. Cash transactions were completely anonymous in nature.

With just a zip code, the retailer would only be able to statistically infer that the person lived nearby or far from that store. They had no physical address, no e-mail address, no anything except a storefront and a sign, and maybe a TV or radio spot or a newspaper ad that might allow them to be proactive in reaching out to push the customer a message. But in terms of reaching individual customers, retailers did nothing. In fact, there wasn't much they could do if they wanted to because they didn't even know who their customers were.

Psychographics is the study of personality, values, opinions, attitudes, interests, and lifestyles. And in terms of customers' psychographic profiles, the industry was in the dark. When thinking about the difference between demographics and psychographics, it's important to note that in the information age, groups are not nearly as homogeneous as in earlier eras. And that's a problem for audience-targeting marketers, who rely heavily on demographics to measure observable variables: sex, race, income, size of household, zip code, etc.

Psychographics, meanwhile, has provided a better way of

segmenting customers by examining the traits people care about, rather than data about them that would appear in a census or survey. Retailers made no effort to learn about their customers except the incidental gathering of some billing zip codes from buyers who happened to pay with a credit card. In a buyer-seller relationship, that disinterest basically smacks of narcissism.

And because of that solipsistic approach, retailers were blind to reality. The industry assumed, even held as gospel, that hardcore hip-hop was a product that sold in inner cities. When it started to sell in volume on college campuses and in suburban regions, retailers were dumbfounded, with no insight as to why it was happening.

The result was that almost all of these industry players eventually ended up with no real customer relationships. The labels had no way to move their customers to new distribution channels. When the retailers lost their grip, the labels had no way to let the Beatles fan who had bought their albums on vinyl, then 8-track, then cassette, and then CD that there was a new way to experience the music. They had lost that customer.

It also meant that every time these format changes happened, the record labels had to reestablish contact with that customer. If they had maintained a long-standing relationship, it would have been much more cost-effective and established loyalty. Instead, the labels had to track down their buyers every time they had something new to sell, demonstrating that they only cared about the customer as a source of revenue.

Furthermore, the labels had partnered with indiscriminate retailers who weren't curators in any sense and who cared nothing about music except to the extent that it furthered the sale of home appliances and electronics. Customers were tired of being in an arranged marriage. So when a better suitor came along, they did just what you would expect: they bolted without hesitation.

In today's highly connected world, with its expectation of transparency and full disclosure, if there is a decline in product quality, there will be a rapid erosion of customer trust in response. And if a company hasn't figured out that it needs to communicate directly with its customers, it might as well search the Yellow Pages to find them, as that method is just as obsolete.

CHAPTER 2

A LITTLE HISTORY

HOW DID WE GET HERE? TO UNDERSTAND THE PROBLEM, WE have to examine it from a macro level. If we take a close look at why all of these problems exist, it's important to make sure that we don't let the inertia and the forces behind those dynamics lead us down the same dangerous path. It's worthwhile to recall some of the history that recounts how we got to this current state.

In the days before the Industrial Revolution, or preindustrialization, economies were localized, with nearby businesses. Much of the commerce that took place happened in a fairly confined geographic region. People who owned most of these businesses lived adjacent to them. Trade was happening across the world, of course, with silk, spices, and precious metals. All these items were being traded across the globe, but most of the day-to-day commerce was very local.

One of the first things that started to change and really challenged the status quo was industrialization because it enabled mass production. Textile manufacturing, steam, and other technological advances might seem trivial today, but in those days, they were revolutionary. As some historians look at the waves that the Industrial Revolution started in the late 1700s, which reverberated all the way into the 1960s, what resulted was the ability to mass produce on a greater scale.

Not that mass production alone is enough to create the dynamics that we see today, but it is one of the key enablers. The ability to mass-produce products paired with mass media is something of a chain reaction in which a mass communication network emerged.

Mass media creates a world where there is an ability to broadcast to a lot of customers simultaneously. And that naturally provides companies with the power to reach entire countries rather than just localized audiences. Mass media creates the ability to communicate the features and benefits of a new product to new markets. Often, these are products consumers never knew they even wanted. They definitely didn't need them, but they were getting introduced to them nevertheless.

There's a famous story about Betty Crocker in which the company found a way to create its cake mix. The new recipe simply required opening the package, adding water, mixing, and putting it in the pan. But consumers felt that they weren't involved enough in the process if they didn't do more. So Betty Crocker changed the formula a bit, requiring people to crack an egg. That extra step of adding an egg was just enough complexity to change the consumer perspective.

Consumers were surprised that they could purchase a home-baked cake in a grocer's aisle. It sounds crazy today to refer to a Betty Crocker cake as homemade, but at that time, the concept of packaged food products was brand new. People had no reference to differentiate between something made at home and something from a box. The product message was that they could get a homemade cake in twenty minutes instead of two hours.

National advertising kicked off what would become national brands. The reason these national brands can exist is because of the combination of mass production and mass media, as companies can create products on a large scale and communicate their message to millions of people at the same time. Rather than buy advertising market by market or an out-of-date model of sponsoring TV shows, they can buy much more cost-effective standardized national ads.

That's an important piece to this puzzle, but one of the more nuanced pieces that isn't as obvious is the evolution of public markets. The ability of companies to go public and gain access to new capital has paved the way for today's modern marketing and consumer culture. Historically, you would go public if your company engaged in business-to-business (B2B) activity. It might be a steel company, like Andrew Carnegie's, in which shares of steel could be purchased, or it might be an energy company, like J. D. Rockefeller's. People could buy shares of this energy stock, and the capital that these companies raised to the public market would help fund their growth.

As those types of companies started to mature, the public market asked what else they could take public because banks, too, realized they could make a lot of money in such endeavors. Banks charged transaction fees, making money each time someone bought or sold shares in a company's stock.

Today, stocks can be traded for less than $5. That's still decent money because the marginal cost to facilitate the trade is almost zero. Before Internet trading, every time stock was traded, a scaling commission was typically paid. Selling one hundred shares versus ten thousand shares came with a different commission. The stock brokers and the banks were highly incentivized to keep people trading these stocks because whether they went up or down, they still made money.

The banks that were fueling much of the growth in the public markets needed something else to grow because these energy companies and these commodities were starting to flatten out. There wasn't as much volume trading, so the bank's growth was slowing down. Crafty bankers looked around and started asking, "Why can't these consumer products corporations become public companies?" The answer was simple: they could.

Once there was mass customization, mass communication, and a national advertising network, brands naturally started to receive national recognition. And with that, there is the ability to justify being a publicly traded consumer brand. For the first time, you have highly sophisticated national companies, that could sell not just to other companies but also to relatively unsophisticated and underinformed individual consumers. This was the first time in history that had ever happened, and it became quite troublesome.

There are two big names worth calling out in this discussion. The first is rooted in the advertising-driven consumer culture that started to emerge in the 1950s and 1960s. Famed businessman Peter Drucker is quoted as saying, "The purpose of a business is to create a customer. And business has only two functions—marketing and innovation." If companies do those two things very well, they will stay in business.

This idea certainly was not lost on the rapidly emerging consumer companies of this time. In parallel, psychology began shaping what would evolve into the field of behavioral science. One of the early pioneers in this space was Edward Bernays, who combined crowd psychology with the psychoanalytical concepts of his influential uncle, Sigmund Freud.

Bernays focused on helping spread messages for consumer product companies, political campaigns, and government outreach. In fact, one of his first achievements was in the field of government outreach, which at the time was simply known as propaganda. Bernays understood the negative connotations the word had acquired, so he renamed it "public relations."

Theorist Abraham Maslow argued that humans have basic needs that need to be fulfilled before higher needs can be met. Max Neef realized that human behavior became more difficult to predict after those basic survival needs were met. Bernays understood both of these concepts and they heavily influenced his work. Bernays also believed that in a prosperous environment, such as the postwar period, humans will manufacture new needs to overcome. This means, of course, that their buying habits will change.

One of the ways that buying habits change for the prosperous is that the purchased product loses luster over time and that the buyer must upgrade to meet the need of getting something new. Marketers, Bernays knew, could exploit this. And so they did, manipulating the inherent need to need by creating an insatiable desire for the next big thing. That was great for a publicly traded company that requires constant growth to make money for its shareholders. However, the ability to create this demand and the necessity to continue growing requires exploiting the consumer.

There is a concept known as the hedonic treadmill, which states that there is a tendency for humans to quickly return to a relatively stable level of happiness despite major positive or negative events or life changes.

An example of this in the context of consumer products is your car. Suppose you're in college and driving a beat-up Nissan Sentra. You graduate and get a new job, and you want to buy a new car, and you long for the Altima, which will make you feel like you've made it. Then, two months after you get a new Altima, the novelty wears off. Now, you're looking at the Infiniti, which offers even more status. Then, a Mercedes-Benz. The joy wears off. The need for better is insatiable. For the consumer, this form of manipulation is a prison of desire from which there seems to be no escape.

But wait, the madness gets even crazier. The US government eventually stepped in, not to regulate the marketing industry or inform consumers but to assist companies in ramping up production and maintaining steady growth. Consumption had become a material part of our economy by the 1950s, but in the 1970s' economic downturn, a number of macroeconomic trends, including unemployment, took root, and the country was threatened by a flood of new goods via globalization and the expansion of free trade into previously closed markets.

The flip side of globalization, however, is that the United States could also ship its products to other countries. Not only could it ship goods abroad, but it could also produce them abroad and at a tremendous savings. In addition to cheaper labor overseas, the import-export laws weren't sophisticated enough at the time to keep up with the pace of that change.

Realizing all of this, the government decided to create better incentives for business. Through subsidies placed earlier in the supply chain, it could help companies continue growing. If the companies could keep growing, they would resultantly keep hiring people, and that would—so the thinking went—keep unemployment low, allow people with jobs to keep buying stuff, and get politicians reelected. It's a circle that keeps going even today.

The plan was well intended rather than some malicious effort to undermine the American people. However, the result had unintended consequences, particularly for certain types of products. A company that made a soft drinks, snacks, or TV dinners, for example, would lobby for a better corn subsidy to make a syrup sweetener cheaper. That would allow it to reduce its cost and continue to up its profit margins. That short-term incentive spurred those companies' behavior, which has the effect of rapidly eroding customer trust.

Worse still are scenarios in which the consumer simply becomes part of the profit formula. The customer is no longer seen as buying the product; the consumer is the product. When companies started putting lower-quality ingredients into their product, the result had to have impact elsewhere. National issues, such as health care, in the form of an obesity epidemic or various cancers, developed into crises. These issues were not coincidentally occurring alongside these new shifts in national policy as it regarded business; they were, as factual data confirm, part and parcel of it.

Just as health-care problems rose, so did consumer debt. The hedonic treadmill, which consumers were unwittingly riding, may have nothing for their waistlines, but it certainly slimmed down their pocketbooks. Ad campaigns convinced Americans that they were unhappy and would not be happy until they bought the latest fill-in-the-blank. Having already spent on their disposable income but still feeling empty, consumers were encouraged to buy now and pay later.

In the 1980s, the system looked fantastic. Corporations were working together. Everyone was doing well, and consumerism was fueling gross domestic product growth in America. But even then, there were no target levels established to stabilize things. It is possible that if companies had slowed their growth at that point and maintained a status quo afterward, the system would have attained a form of equilibrium, and I wouldn't be writing this book. Obviously, that's not what happened. The business world believed that if it grew 5 percent last year, it could and should grow 6 percent the next.

This, as you're probably realizing, is the plot for every movie about Wall Street. Companies feel the need to grow perpetually, like sharks that must continue to move. In the 1980s, the pressure for growth became overwhelming. Instead of making better products, public companies optimized for growth rather than customer satisfaction. It looked like the new normal.

At that time, there weren't data to know how bad things were and how many consumers were being exploited. In the same way that music retailers kept humming a tune as they moved forward, never bothering to track their customers, business kept juicing on steroids, never looking to see if anyone was being crushed underfoot.

But things changed. The Internet arrived on the scene—a caped superhero to some, a Bond villain to others. The whole system started to topple as people became empowered in a way that was never possible before. In the new information age, and specifically the Internet era (kicking off about 1995), consumers started to have more purchasing information—not quite 100 percent but certainly new information to which they had never before had access. And they shared that information with each other freely.

This new level of transparency is not just for academics or people in the industries who have been acutely paying attention. The masses began to realize they were getting duped and that companies had been selling them products that weren't nearly as great as the advertisement promised. At the same time, this new transparency revealed that executives were being compensated like kings, even as wages continued to stagnate and households required two earners. These discrepancies spawned a wave of skepticism and cynicism and began to destroy public trust in corporate America like never before.

For many companies, the brand loyalty they'd worked so hard to earn was quickly discarded. Winning back that trust would never be so simple again or as cheap. The tone-deaf response by business was to get savvier marketing teams and channel their inner Edward Bernays, manufacturing a better class of customer needs. It never dawned on them that the jig was up, that their customers were on to them.

When thinking about designing businesses today, companies can't market their way to growth if the product is broken. The genie can never be put back into the bottle. It's not that the old way is being reshaped; it's that it is, in fact, dying. It will soon be extinct. You are reading about it as it unravels; your grandchildren will hear about it as history.

Once bitten, twice shy. Consumers, once victims of ignorance, will never again allow themselves the innocence and naïveté their parents and grandparents displayed at the hands of men like Bernays. Modern consumers will gather ever more information as they become increasingly sophisticated.

In a world in which customers have near-perfect information, they're going to demand that companies build quality products and have authentic conversations with them. The bait-and-switch routine is over. And customers will walk away if they don't feel they can trust a company. To compete in the world as it exists today requires a new approach to business design.

CHAPTER 3

THE SOLUTION

WHEN LOOKING AT WHAT BUSINESS DESIGN FOR HIGH-growth companies looks like today, one of the first things to tackle is how consumers are influenced by products. There are three primary ways in which a product's value can be discovered.

Historically, the leading factors in a consumer's decision to purchase were, in order of importance, trusted experts, personal experience, and social circle. And those trusted experts, who act as proxies for the consumer, were by far the most critical factor. Today, those proxies are at the bottom of the list in terms of influence. Meanwhile, the people in one's social circle are now easily the most persuasive.

Consumers don't trust much of today's marketing messages. A study done by the Yankelowich Group showed that more than 75 percent of consumers don't believe that companies are telling the truth in their advertising. This is important to note because it means that a portion of potential customers being reached with an advertising campaign won't believe it no matter how clearly the message is articulated.

On the other side of this, some of the customers who may be more receptive to an advertising campaign have to sort out if they believe the brand or not. They have to figure out how to digest the message. When friction or complexity is introduced to the decision process, the consumer will often shut down and not make a decision. In the case of a new product or service, it means they likely will not adopt or purchase the product. Companies need to tackle this problem head-on.

The problem for companies is getting into the consumer's social circle. You can't show up once in a while and expect someone to be engaged with your brand. You have to authentically and consistently show up. If companies are not able to pull that off, or don't have the right model to do that, customers just aren't going to trust them.

Companies are starting to recognize that this is the new normal, but they aren't doing enough. It's common for product teams and third-party agencies to conduct focus groups to better understand their potential customers and help shape the products they build. But focus groups aren't enough. There are a couple of reasons why these tools aren't satisfactory by themselves.

First, it's expensive to implement. It requires full-time employees or hired agencies. Not even large companies can afford to staff this capability at massive scale. As a result, the company must ask when the appropriate time is in the product life cycle in which to pay for this type of work.

Second, these models rely on secondary sources rather than getting it straight from the horse's mouth. These exercises don't continually observe the behavior around the actual product or activity; instead, they focus on understanding the gap between someone's underlying values and his or her behaviors. Often, what people say they do and what they actually do are disconnected. That disconnection is something that marketers would traditionally exploit.

Marketers need to figure out what they are actually trying to test. Are they trying to exploit the difference between their customers' behavior and the attitudes, or are they trying to improve their relationship with their customers? The latter is the most critical, but when dealing with the aforementioned proxies, this method is flawed because many times, they're not observing the true activity but just getting survey answers.

Consider a company planning to build a new piece of software designed to do a better job of managing the wall calendar in the kitchen of a customer's home. The software company may hire an agency to recruit a panel of potential customers and ask, "How often do you change the events on your calendar or make updates? How many people participate in this activity?"

The challenge here is that they're expecting this potential customer to not only think of this hypothetical question but to also articulate it. They're sometimes even asked to extrapolate what other people like them might think. And while there are statistical models to help make these findings more scientifically accurate, this is still a broken process.

Additionally, when resource constrained, researchers may do a poor job finding the representative for their target demographic or psychographic audience. On the demographic side, these are going to be such things as age, income, race, location, and so forth, which are objective and easier to measure. As mentioned in the previous chapter, psychographics pertains to preferences, so it's very important to receive high-confidence answers from individuals when doing this type of research.

So with the calendar example, the very real challenge you might end up with is someone who answers the question to the best of his or her ability but not understanding the question. Or worse, that answer may be applied to the wrong audience. Digging deeper in that example, one reason it's much better to observe the activity in its natural state is because you are going to see things the potential customer never even thought to mention.

Furthermore, a researcher and a consumer might not be on the same page about the meaning of a key term. The word *calendar*, to go back to the example, might, for the person being asked about it, mean something with a scenic picture on top and a list of dates beneath it but functioning more as a piece of art than a functional time-tracking device. That person might place sticky notes on the fridge as reminders about meetings, errands, or whatever.

Now, if researchers never connected those two pieces, they wouldn't know to dig deeper. It could turn out that what the customer does with the sticky notes on the fridge is exactly the problem the new software is trying to solve. If you can observe that, you might get better insights.

Another common misstep with traditional user research is failure to accurately model the frequency of the usage. Successful business models are increasingly service based, for example, advertising, microtransaction, subscription. So completing the calendar software and convincing customers to install it isn't enough.

In a world in which the value exchange is increasingly spread across time, it's very difficult to build high-growth products that aren't used on a recurring basis. It's not enough to simply get people to start using a product; they need to keep using it. Many times, traditional user-research activities are not extracting the right answers to ensure that value is delivered in a sustainable manner. There are design researchers who navigate all of this exceptionally well. There are others who really don't, and the variance between those two is vast.

Finally, there are flaws with this proxy method that are similar to the telephone game. An agency is often going to recruit a sample of the target audience. The answers that those researchers get to their questions are going to then get summarized into some type of report that is presented to the brand manager, designer, product manager, or similar role, and they're going to digest the insights and go back to the core product team to improve the product based on the feedback.

There are a lot of steps and a number of places where the core insight can be manipulated or exaggerated in the wrong direction, even by accident. It's best to find the most direct relationship between the customer and the team actually building the product. Don't depend on someone else or a process as a replacement for direct communication.

Businesses should be treating their customer relationships the same way they would treat a good personal relationship. We would find it odd if someone only spoke to his or her spouse or partner every forty-five days and through a counselor. That would be an odd way to maintain a relationship with someone you care about. It should not be surprising that brand affinity tends to be low for products or services that only speak to their customers infrequently and through proxy channels as part of a transactional relationship.

The frequency and the authenticity of the conversations with a customer are really important, and that is one reason that the processes we use to get actionable customer insights are suboptimal.

One of the first actions companies need to take is engaging in smaller, more frequent exchanges of value. By this I mean finding smaller ways to exchange the product value for the customer's time and money in a way that lowers the perceived risk. In the early part of the relationship, the amount of time and money that a customer is willing to invest with a brand is probably going to be low until trust is established. That's key because without trust, the frequency of the communication can't be increased, and it will never get to the point where the relationship feels authentic.

In the video game industry, there are still a lot of people who buy *Call of Duty* for PlayStation or Xbox. They pay $59. The game publisher has built a highly engaged customer audience. However, it can take two years to build this type of product. The game publisher is banking a lot on where the customers will be and what they will want pretty far into the future. It's a risky business, and as a result, there aren't many tier-one or AAA franchise titles on game consoles. It's also why it's rare for a new large-budget video game franchise to be released.

Something similar happens in the movie industry. Audiences continually complain about all the sequels that are released. While the studios may try to create original content, they get penalized if audiences don't feel a relationship with that brand, so audiences are not willing to spend the increasingly more expensive cost of admission plus snacks or waste two to three hours of precious time. The predictability of the sequel, however, reduces the perceived risk in the decision. There is built-in trust in the brand.

The video game industry would love it if the billions of people using smartphones would purchase $59 games. They don't. In fact, it's increasingly difficult to convince players to even pay $0.99 before playing a casual game on a phone. This is similar to what we saw with music. People want the product but are refusing to pay for the value in advance. Casual video games like *Candy*

Crush capitalize on this by giving the basic game away for free and charging to unlock value as the customer continues to play the game. These small transactions are called microtransactions.

There are typically two types of microtransactions in games. One is called cosmetic, or personalization, in which the purchase doesn't really help performance in the game but may provide some social status. That could be a digital T-shirt with your favorite sports team's logo that you buy for your character. The other popular type of microtransaction helps user progress through the game faster than normal. Sometimes it's called paying to win. You might hear a hard-core gamer ask, "Are you paying to win or are you grinding it out?"

Certain gamers have an aversion to games that allow people to pay to win. It can be considered unfair. If someone ends up on the leaderboard but paid for half of those levels, some would say it's not equitable and takes the fun out of the game for others.

Throughout this example, what's most interesting is that if a player never decides to pay for a cosmetic or a game progression microtransaction, he or she can still keep playing the game. Companies have conditioned consumers to understand this approach. For brands that people don't have relationships with, it's a fantastic way to start the conversation. In a relationship context, it's akin to dating.

Starting a customer relationship is like dating someone new. People don't go on a first date and expect to jump on a plane and fly to Paris together. Grabbing coffee, on the other hand, is an example of an interaction that starts to build trust. And it's not just the opportunity for good conversation that can be had over coffee, but all the little interactions that signal whether or not the other person is trustworthy: does that person make eye contact, reveal an appropriate amount of personal information, share the same values, and so on? Trust is important because it becomes a way to forecast how that relationship will pan out in the future.

Again, trust is the ability to predict future behavior. So if companies don't create opportunities to build trust, they're going to be limited to just microtransactions. They will never get to the opportunities where there's enough trust extended that they can create an exchange on a large scale. That becomes a problem because if people don't trust them, they will only exchange value if the investment is small and the risk is low.

The unfortunate thing for anxious brands, especially those trying to build high-growth products, is that there's no shortcut to building trust. They want to believe they can drive an advertising campaign that delivers an emotional connection in a manner that accelerates the maturity of the relationship. However, trust is not earned in that way; in fact, it's a really poor way of trying to win the heart of the customer.

The attempt to hurry the relationship actually has two strange effects. First, it requires a lot of transactions to make the money companies need to stay in business. In a dating relationship, it would be the equivalent of getting coffee every day. At some point, the other person is going to think the relationship is only about coffee.

Worse, more and more small transactions are required to sustain the business model and achieve growth. So, in terms of a dating relationship, you're not even sitting down and having a conversation over coffee at some point; you're just getting it to go and saying good-bye. Whether in a business or a personal relationship, this type of relationship eventually becomes financially untenable because one party is continually spending money on the other and getting nothing substantial in return, just the potential promise of the next interaction.

Mobile games, again, provide a good example of what that type of relationship looks like in business. Inside mobile games, and mobile apps in general, there are some well-known metrics used to understand how companies are building relationships with their customers. One is the cost per install, which is the amount of money a company needs to spend on advertising to get someone to install an application. That varies widely, but on iOS (the operating system that runs or powers iPhones and iPads) and Android, there are data that show how much companies are spending on average. Because of the competition in mobile apps and games, it costs a lot.

Fisku is a company that tracks mobile usage across a number of metrics. It tracks a metric called cost per loyal user (CPLU), which is the amount it costs to acquire a customer who is likely to remain loyal. The CPLU for an Android or iOS app varies each month, usually in the range of $2 to $5 per user. And that's an expensive way to get customers.

Let's assume a company sets a goal of one million customers. Let's say further that it is getting a low CPLU of $2.50. That means the company would be paying $2.5 million in cash for the acquisition. Bear in mind that cost does nothing to guarantee those customers will continue to use the app after it is installed.

These aren't soft, abstract numbers; these are real dollars that would be wired to some company to get this to happen. That number is driven largely by the price of advertising within other apps where the ideal customer is already spending time. It's a genuine dice roll. As previously stated, more than three quarters of people ignore or do not trust ads. So you know going in that much of the money you're spending—in this instance, $2.5 million—is going right out the window.

That money will result in some people installing the app. Now, at the same time you are looking for more people to install it, you have to manage to retain the customers you just found. One metric that measures how you keep customers is N-day retention—the percentage of customers who come back and perform any action in your product "N" days after they start using it. Common intervals to measure N-day retention are one day, three days, seven days, and twenty-right days. These are the windows in which you have the greatest chance to keep a new customer.

Spend enough money and you'll get people to try your product. But if you don't deliver real value and haven't invested in authentic relationships, customers won't stay. Even really great products have customers who "churn," or eventually move on from it. In the 1980s, Sony dominated the portable music industry with its Walkman. Eventually, though, practically all of its customers churned out and moved over to Apple, which offered a more convenient product in the form of digital media.

However, just because customers will churn out doesn't mean they have to necessarily leave the brand. Back then, a music listener might have started with a Sony transistor radio, then moved on to a Sony boom box, and then the Walkman. If Sony had kept innovating, it might have produced an MP3 player that was the next logical progression for their customers.

Instead, the company created the Sony Walkman CD player, which was even larger than the original. Moreover, because of the delicate nature of CDs, it was rather useless for the rough-and-tumble activities in which customers wanted to use it; in reality, CDs were just a more expensive and more fragile form of the cassette player, albeit one with better sound quality. At that point, people wanted a product that played digital music. (That didn't even last very long, as smartphones entered the market only a few years later and put a nail in the coffin of the dedicated music player.)

Companies have to be very cognizant of how they're

maintaining customer relationships because as the market changes, the perceived needs of the customer changes as well. Those needs are much easier to identify when companies and their customers are having authentic ongoing conversations.

It's not like anyone needed a digital music player to survive in the world. It's not a building block on Maslow's pyramid, but it is something that people value. If a company is not paying attention to how those needs are shifting, even if the needs are perceived by the customer, its customers are going to leave.

Now the company is stuck with having to fight to get customers again. It should be pointed out that the cost of keeping a customer is much lower than the cost of gaining a new customer. Although it varies across industries, in the mobile app space I've been discussing, according to Bain (one of the world's leading management consulting companies), the cost of acquiring a new customer is six to seven times higher than the cost of retaining an existing customer.

That said, most companies are laser focused on acquiring new customers, so even as they gain a new customer, they begin neglecting that person immediately. It's a horrible way to do business. The point here is that keeping customers is one of the most important things a company can focus on as a success metric. Retention is a measure of trust, which makes it a useful piece of datum and a natural place to invest, as that trust ensures growth for the simple reason that a loyal customer will buy other products or services that you make available.

Without trust, your customers aren't going to take a chance on the rest of your product line, which means you are missing a prime opportunity with your own customer base.

In retail, there's a popular management tool called Net Promoter Score (NPS) that measures the loyalty between a provider and a customer. While useful, NPS doesn't provide enough detail to measure whether that loyalty translates into daily or weekly usage of a product. That level of detail is increasingly valuable in predicting how and when a customer will give his or her time to a product. Without that information, it's difficult to know how much to charge for the product and where to place the cash register. Every product must choose its core business model and determine where in the experience the business model will surface—that is, where you place the cash register.

There's an acronym that condenses a number of business models into four big categories: FAST, which stands for Free, Ad- and sponsorship-supported, Subscription, and Transactional revenue.

What does that mean?

Free simply means giving away a product to build a relationship. It might mean subsidizing the product by taking a loss on it in an effort to monetize it or another product at another time, or to offer a sample of what the customer can expect from the rest of the product line.

Years ago, Mercedes-Benz reached out to music producers and songwriters, requesting to license music for a flat fee in exchange for website visitors having the ability to download the music from Mercedes at no cost. It wanted to create a better relationship with its customers, which entailed receiving contact information as a prerequisite to getting the music.

It also compensated the artists while helping them build their fan base at the same time. It was a win-win situation. The result of this was that the customer perceived this service as free, but in reality, what was happening was the groundwork of a customer relationship. Free was the doorway to a new relationship.

Another way that free surfaces in the marketplace is in the services that are called freemium, which means that some of the services are given away for free so customers can become accustomed to the product before deciding it's a product relationship they want. Over time, there are other ways to sell to the customer. Many software-as-a-service (SaaS) applications work in this manner, in which the basic tier is free, and over time, they sell something else (such as a paid subscription referenced later on). In-app purchases and microtransactions are common business models to monetize freemium software experiences. Free is a key business model pillar, but it usually works in combination with other products and services.

The second in the FAST acronym is advertising/sponsorships. These are experiences in which a third-party brand or service advertises or subsidizes the product or service. The classic example of this is broadcast television or radio in the form of a commercial break. In the golden era of television, this was more of a sponsorship model. Soap operas are so named because soap manufacturing companies and similar brands would sponsor radio and television shows. The entire show would be sponsored by that brand.

Over time, TV stations found that if they could standardize a smaller unit of creative content, they could make more money for the same window of time. Rather than sell just one to three sponsorships, they started packaging video advertisements in fifteen-, thirty-, or sixty-second slots. This is why there are odd ratios of broadcast time: a thirty-minute episode will only run about twenty-two minutes with the remaining time given to commercials. Similarly, a sixty-minute program may consist of only forty-four minutes of the show peppered with sixteen minutes of advertisements.

Advertising is a well-known business model. The biggest challenge for the ad-supported experience is that it needs extreme scale, such as single-digit millions or tens of millions of customers to receive any significant payoff. Either that or they need a huge amount of customer data within a specific demographic in order to pull off effective targeted messaging.

Prescription drug ads, for instance, particularly those that are applicable to only a niche audience, aren't generally broadcast during prime time, at least on the major networks, because that's a lot of money to spend to reach a small amount of potential customers. The 6:00 p.m. nightly news, however, which draws a significant elderly audience, is chock-full of ads for drugs that fight arthritis, high cholesterol, and of course, erectile dysfunction.

Because this target demographic flocks to a particular network at a particular time, it is a reliable commodity for pharmaceutical companies that are willing to pay high rates to reach a dense concentration of likely customers.

Demographics are what are observable about people. They include details such as age, ethnicity, and zip code. The psychographic profile is more of a clustering of interests, such as political leanings, favorite type of pizza or genre of music. If companies can build a better psychographic profile, they are not limited by something as ultimately unhelpful as a zip code, which will encompass too wide a swath of different types to target with any degree of precision. This is especially important as urban density continues to bring more people to more concentrated metropolitan areas.

Marketers are now starting to understand that it's not enough to simply move from demographic to psychographic marketing; they also have to give up the old assumption that there are, in fact, large, homogeneous customer segments. Just because one person likes to go hiking doesn't mean that person prefers a certain brand of granola bar. The more we learn about customers, the more we learn how individualized each one is in his or her own particular needs and desires. Taken to its logical extension, every customer is, in the final analysis, as unique as a snowflake.

Advertising remains one of the better ways to broadcast messages in a wide manner, but it's highly inefficient. Targeted ads are going to become a more critical component in all types of advertising, whether through print, broadcast, or digital.

The third item in the FAST acronym is subscription. This is a largely recurring revenue stream. It can be a set amount, as with a newspaper delivery, or it can fluctuate based on usage, like an electricity bill, which is metered, so the amount due each month varies but is paid for on a monthly basis. There is typically a fixed cost to keep the service on, and then there are prices per kilowatt hour of energy used in a given period. Even though these are not fixed prices, they are absolutely considered subscriptions.

The recurring nature of these subscriptions provides predictable revenue streams for those types of businesses. Out of the four business models, the goal or aspiration is to find a service that has low customer acquisition cost, high retention, and a recurring revenue stream. It might not work out perfectly, but these three attributes help develop a durable business model.

It should be noted that subscriptions come in many forms. Netflix is an example of a subscription service that charges a flat rate plus tax each month. These are recurring services and therefore, must continually deliver clear value to stay in business. With any subscription, it's almost guaranteed that a customer believes he or she needs or strongly desires to have that service in his or her life. A gas or electric bill is needed to stay cool/warm and power appliances and devices. A cell phone is necessary for communication. Even Internet services may be bundled into that.

All of these companies are delivering value twenty-four hours a day. It doesn't mean people are guaranteed to watch Netflix every day, but they have the option to watch a selection of movies and TV shows at any time. The value proposition feels fair and compelling, so companies are given permission from the customer to keep that relationship ongoing.

If a company doesn't have a business model that's free, advertising based, or subscription based, it may not be a true service-based experience. If it's not service based, it becomes more difficult to retain customers over an extended period.

The last item of FAST is transactional, which simply means paying for a value exchange at a given time, and that's that, the transaction is over. Examples of this would be buying groceries or buying a hot dog from a street vendor downtown. Perhaps it's buying a $0.99 app. Transactional business models are still important and aren't going anywhere despite the alternatives.

If someone purchases a car rather than leasing it, that's a transaction. In markets such as the auto industry that have been stable since the industry began, there are companies exploring new business models. For instance, Lyft is partnering with GM to build a fleet of self-driving cars, the premise being that there are going to be fewer people in the future who want the headaches and hassles that come with car ownership. This may be especially true for millennials who will become the foundation of the economic base in the future and will most likely crop up first in very dense metropolitan areas. What Lyft is looking to develop is a subscription-based car service, where for a certain amount of money per month, a customer would receive a specific number of miles or amount of time for that particular car service.

When looking at these four business model pillars, notice how many companies in the world have been optimizing for the one-and-done nature of the transactional revenue. One of the key reasons for this is that they don't have great relationships with their customers. They've ended up with this model that costs a lot to keep finding paths to reengage that customer to get him or her to buy the next thing. They require a lot of promotions and a lot of advertising.

Imagine a grocery store customer. Some people will drink Coca-Cola and no other brand, so there is some loyalty in that regard. However, people increasingly tend to prefer a category rather than a brand. Do they want a carbonated beverage at all? Are they looking to make sure it doesn't include ingredients like high-fructose corn syrup and aspartame, or do they prefer sugar cane? From there, they may break it down into flavor profile—cola, root beer, lemon-lime, and so on—to winnow it down.

Often, because of the sequencing of how customers are making those decisions, it puts brands in a tough position. If a non-brand-loyal customer, maybe a millennial who hasn't made a deep attachment, walks into a store looking for a diet lemon-lime soda and does not care which particular brand it is, that buyer may simply settle for whatever is on sale. In this process, brands have now trained their customers to buy their products only when they are on sale.

In so doing, that brand is now in perpetual sales motion, unable by law to collude with competitors to divvy up the market by coordinating sales prices and, all the while, unable to provide any value in addition to the core product.

These companies are stuck in a bad position because any time they compete on price, they have to seek out other ways to save money. That's one of the reasons why, in the beverage space, the sweetener is such a divisive issue. No matter where you sit concerning certain sweeteners, the reason there are alternatives is because the beverage companies continually have had to rely on running promotions, and those promotions have to be paid for while trying to maintain profit margins.

The reason all of this exists is because they haven't taken the right approach on building a real relationship with the customer. They've relied primarily on so-called lifestyle marketing, consisting of aspirational images and slick, well-produced commercials that seduce customers into wanting to mimic what they see. The underlying point is that companies have put themselves in a position where the margin they make per customer continues to shrink.

Looking at these four business models in the FAST acronym, there's nothing prescriptive that says one is necessarily better than the other. However, advertising and subscription-based business models are better signals, or mapped more closely, to the service world, where the value to the customer is delivered over a sustained period.

In the mobile app and gaming world, two common metrics used are ARPU and ARPPU. ARPU is the average revenue per user over a given period. Typically, it's measured per month or per year. ARPPU, on the other hand, is the average revenue that a company makes per paying user. The distinction is important because companies want an easy ramp for people to try their products before they take their money. Some of those customers are going to be using the product and not giving the company money, which costs the company. Therefore, they need to be able to normalize the ARPU for both people who never gave any money, as well as a separate metric on the average revenue made for the specific people who did give money.

From there, they can compare those two types to understand whether there is a freeloader problem or a cost structure that can't be sustained. Usually, these challenges are connected because a company is not driving enough value to convert its target customers, or it's chasing the wrong customer segment. The takeaway is that companies are on a journey and they're moving customers through a funnel to build a more authentic relationship.

The flaw with how the customer funnel is being managed today is that too many companies are optimizing for the top of the funnel. They're spending ridiculous amounts of money to acquire customers with almost no long-term view on how they will keep them. Part of that is because these consumer companies are under the pressures that come with being a public company, which must continue to grow. They must show results on a quarterly basis, which means progress every three months. They're not optimizing for where the relationship is going to be.

It's an awful way to do business because at some point, the company's cost of capital is going to exceed the cost it takes to get and keep those customers. This behavior persists despite there being a well-known model around the relationship between the customer acquisition cost and the customer lifetime value.

Suppose, for example, I get a home equity loan for 5 percent, and I do something to improve my house. There's a pretty clear calculation that shows whether the new kitchen will improve the value of the home. A kitchen remodel usually does improve the value of the home, but this forced appreciation doesn't typically cover the full cost of the remodel. Homeowners justify this by attributing additional value to the intangible benefits they believe they or a future homeowner will place on the remodel.

It's bad math, but the homeowner still justifies the decision. In our personal lives, we make irrational decisions all the time, and we place a lot of value on the emotional payoff around the costs that are more difficult to calculate.

For businesses, however, it doesn't make sense to make emotional decisions. The math has to be there. It costs money to make money, and the ratio between those two needs to be properly managed in order to stay in business. The balancing act between those two is even more challenging for a high-growth product that has to grow quickly using finite resources: people, money, and time.

Let's take a look at another example. Most adults in the United States have a smartphone. If you consume media—whether it be cable, broadcast networks, the Internet, or even the radio—you can't escape the constant fighting between the mobile telecommunications companies. Each of the top four players in the game—whether it be AT&T, Sprint, T-Mobile, or Verizon—claims its product is better, its rates are better, or they care more about you. Each has its own distinct marketing approach, but they're all saying something very similar about a very similar product.

These four majors and their subsidiaries comprise the bulk of the market. This is an industry that is guilty of the faulty practices listed above. Their focus is on acquiring new customers; their metric for success is growing their customer acquisition velocity. They assume, of course, that they will just keep their current customers despite doing anything special to invest in them. This is an industry optimized for the top of the funnel.

The customer-acquisition cost for a US-based mobile customer, though there are tiers and different segments, are largely focused on what we call postpaid phone subscribers. They are the ones who receive a bill that includes the cost of what they've already used, as opposed to a customer with a prepaid phone plan who pays for use in advance. The carriers have figured out that even the customer with the lowest ARPU is still worth at least $250, so they are willing to spend $250 in cash to get this customer. With certain channels and customer segments, that number can reach as high as $600. So if someone is an AT&T user, one of the other three competitors is willing to spend between $250 and $600 to convince that person to switch services.

The problem now is that the customer is being conditioned to looking at the service in a transactional manner, instead of establishing a brand relationship. What ends up happening is that growth starts to contract for one of those three players. If Sprint gets that customer, the other three are now also in play for that same customer. A year or two later, when a new phone hits the market and there are new pricing options, the customer may decide T-Mobile is a better fit.

Sprint is in danger of having now potentially lost that customer to T-Mobile. These companies are under tremendous pressure to grow, and as a result, they start to get more aggressive on their customer-acquisition spending. They might decide to increase their customer-acquisition threshold up to $700 without supporting data to prove that's the right number. But increasingly, they aren't able to keep their customer long enough to justify the initial cost spent acquiring that customer. The math doesn't work, and over time, the capital markets won't provide them enough money in either equity or debt to subsidize the shell game they've been playing. They are effectively kicking a can down the road and have not focused on the true long-term value of the customer relationship.

Over time, in this industry, the service will have to fundamentally change to address this dysfunction. One of the reasons this issue exists is because the companies have allowed their products to be viewed as commodities. And the nature of commodities is that one is fairly indistinguishable from another.

Take gold or oil, for instance. Both are valuable commodities. Experts in those industries could probably differentiate the particular quality or variety of those substances and perhaps determine where in the world they were extracted. But to you and me, gold's gold and oil's oil. They're interchangeable. And that's exactly what has happened to the offerings that the mobile telecoms have provided. They've been commodified.

By being laser focused on snatching up new customers, they've neglected the relationships they're currently in. And it's that model that still drives most businesses. It's capital intensive and results in diminishing returns over time. It's also counterintuitive to the way that most investors think when they buy an equity or a share of stock in a public company. They're not seeking out risk unless there's a comparable upside. However, the risk-versus-reward ratio for many public companies is not properly reflected in the company's share price.

Much of the rationale in following this flawed customer acquisition–focused strategy is rooted in the assumption that access to that capital will keep flowing in perpetuity. But whether you're a private company or a public one, at some point, you'll run out of sources for new cash. And if you bet your whole business on that structure, the very thing that once functioned as a competitive advantage will be its downfall. When investors get comfortable with a certain level of return, and when the amount of resources required to get that return increases, they're going to be unhappy.

So, if this strategy is indeed flawed, what is a company to do? The answer to that question is what forms the core of this book. The proposal for the alternate path is what I call Values-Based Business Design, and its foundation is based on two simple and actionable elements: listen to the consumer and deliver value every twenty-four hours.

Over the remainder of this book, I'm going to get into more depth on how to execute on that rule set. Similar to great health and fitness, this rule set is something that requires a real process, real motivation, and real conviction. But if you follow this plan, you will have amazing results. Your brand, products, and services will be in their best shape possible, which is what you want to aspire to.

Let me begin by clarifying some terms. Listening to the consumer requires understanding your customers' value system and aligning it with the product, brand, or the company's value system. The only way you're going to be able to do that is to actually engage with real people in authentic ways, which is also the way to sustain the relationship.

When I say values, I'm talking about the essence of what defines an individual and the things that person stands for. It's those things you want populating your personal world: the people, the products, the environment. If a company can't articulate exactly what those things are, it won't be able to align with them. This is true of small, family-run operations and *Fortune* 500s.

As in life, so in business, you can't buy love. Instead, you have to build relationships and maintain them much the way that a gardener tends to a beloved rosebush, seeing that it gets just enough sunshine and a proper amount of water.

So who is tending to its relationships among today's businesses? Slack, for one. Slack is a company that makes professional software, consolidating the conversations that happen in the workplace into a single shared experience.

Elsewhere, those conversations are happening in disaggregated form via e-mail in which two people have a conversation, then maybe loop in the rest of the office in a CC. A chain of e-mails ensues, but any party who isn't directly interested has stopped paying attention. When someone is asked why he or she didn't perform a task that was "in the e-mail," that person can only reply that he or she didn't think he or she was still involved in the conversation anymore. Inboxes are stuffed to the gills with new messages that will never be read.

Slack, on the other hand, has built a product that allows those conversations to happen within a central location, which is online or on a mobile app, rather than buried in e-mail. It's simplified the interaction model to just the rudimentary basics. It's not full of gimmicks or extras that no one will actually ever use but that look good on paper. Instead, it has put together a stripped-down product that is taut, including only the essentials. It doesn't have a ton of features, but those it does have are smooth and polished.

In my past history as a consultant, clients would ask why their campaigns weren't resonating with customers. One of the flaws I consistently saw was that many of these campaigns tended to have a very company- or product-centric view of the world. In reality, a company's offerings are small components of a very heterogeneous mix of products and services in people's lives. Once you get comfortable with that reality, it's easier to understand that people don't need thirty random features in a single product.

Commercial software or B2B apps that streamline efficiency today are what we call SaaS companies, which typically charge a recurring subscription fee. They're a far cry from the old boxed software that companies used to use. There was a time when this was very expensive because it required a lot of people getting on airplanes and traveling from city to city to convince the CIOs of this company or that why this software was going to save the day. Lawyers would be brought in, terms negotiated, contracts drawn up, consultants brought in, and IT professionals sent to actually implement the software. By the time this process was completed, it might be two or three, maybe even five, years down the road, and that CIO might be working somewhere else, the industry might have shifted, or any number of issues might have occurred that invalidated the whole process.

As if in response to that bureaucratic nightmare, Slack figured out that by creating a product that was much more limited in scope, it could provide an easy ramp to try the product, while at the same time, it could focus on honing to perfection the smaller set of capabilities it chose to offer. In so doing, the company severely reduced the cost of customer acquisition to the tens of dollars, down from what was $100 to $200 per user in a typical commercial software sell.

Slack is scaling to a wide number of companies very quickly because the product is easy to set up. So easy, in fact, that ordinary, non-IT professionals can sign up and start using it. And it's reliable. It is a product people are using every day, so when they get software bugs or something is broken, there are clear channels to provide customer feedback, which it collects, fixes, and quickly rolls out to all customers in real time, whereas with the old software, you had to wait until next year's update for the bug fix.

By looking at certain analytics, the team at Slack can determine implicitly where people are getting stuck and see which features aren't being used. Simultaneously, they respond in real time to explicit complaints or suggestions when something is broken or doesn't work optimally, so they can prioritize items and address them in the order that will deliver the most impact.

And there's our two axioms right there: listen to the consumer and provide value every twenty-four hours. Because of that, Slack hasn't had to do much advertising. It doesn't have to. Most of the company's early customers were acquired through word of mouth. It has developed real relationships by providing something of value rather than artificial relationships by throwing money into marketing.

While Slack has had early success, it's now faced with pressure to grow, which has caused the company to start exploring traditional customer-growth options, such as TV ads. It will be interesting to see how the company balances the quality of its customer relationships while taking advantage of its early explosive growth.

Regardless of how you're influenced by a product—your personal experience, social circle, or proxy marketing advertising channels—you're trying to figure out whether that source can be trusted for that particular decision. The power of earned media and word of mouth is that people rarely go out of their way to cosign a product that they don't have a financial or personal relationship with. As a result, when someone tells the customer he or she should try a product, it's powerful. The only reason a person would make a recommendation is because that influencer feels the product warrants the risking of prized social capital.

Companies that put the product first and using whatever they can—whether it's traditional advertising, earned media, or any other type of amplifying tactic—should only be amplifying products that have proven to be great. You have to earn it.

Again, we shouldn't think that advertising is bad, but you have to have a great product, and you get that great product by listening to your customers and understanding how your values align with theirs. You need to build features and benefits that align with your customers' values, and once you do that, advertising is a fantastic way to fuel to the flame of something you already know works.

When going back to examples of the failed big-box stores such as Circuit City, one of the missteps the record labels made was that they allowed the retailer to own the customer relationship. They didn't have an e-mail address, a mailing address, a phone number, or any other type of contact information. That's shameful. In some cases, they might have had a fan club, but they didn't have contact information for the casual music listener who went and purchased a CD at Circuit City in the 1990s. Labels totally ignored the value of maintaining a direct customer relationship. And they paid the price for it.

It's not just that you have to have at least one customer communication channel, you need to own it. Many consumer companies sell their products through retailers. This means that if they can't own the communication channel at the point of retail, they must look at other options. One of the obvious places is social media. But today, this requires a broader and more sophisticated use of the medium than simply as a broadcast mechanism to introduce new products or features. Social media has become a place where real conversations can take place.

Another place where companies can build relationships is in customer service. This is an important way to talk to customers. For many companies, customer service is the channel people use when the product is broken. Handling a customer complaint is a fantastic time to ask real questions because customers are highly incentivized to talk when they're frustrated. And just as in personal relationships, sometimes people need to get things off of their chest. Once that conversation starts, all sorts of hidden issues surface.

Today, many call centers and e-mail help desks are treated as "cost centers," and it's a cost companies are trying reduce as much as possible. What they should be looking at is a customer relationship end point, so they shouldn't be incentivizing those at the call center to spend less time. They should be using that time to learn more about the customer. When done well, these end points become feedback loops to help create better future products.

When I was in graduate school working on my first master's degree, I worked for a company called MicroAge. It's what was called a value-added reseller. In addition to selling computer hardware and software, it provided call-center support for technical companies. This was before a lot of that work was outsourced or offshored to other countries. It hired college students to answer phones for its clients, and at the time, its big client was Apple, Inc., back when it was Apple Computer. This was during the era that Apple was losing its way in the mid-1990s. Apple was manufacturing computers that consumers felt were overpriced but remained invaluable for scenarios such as digital media production.

At MicroAge, we were the toll-free number on the back of the computer manual or box. If you bought a Macintosh computer and something wasn't going right, you would call us. Your phone call would be routed to me in a sea of cubicles, and I'd walk you through a decision tree to help solve your problem as quickly as possible. MicroAge was hyperfocused on productivity. We were given metered thirty-minute lunch breaks and three-minute restroom breaks, and because of that, the call center agents who lasted became highly efficient at reducing call times. We were rewarded for this efficiency.

In hindsight, we shouldn't have been rewarded at all. We should've had a different set of success criteria, one in which we tried to learn more about the customer who called us.

One day I was on a call, and a guy was frustrated because the software he installed was not showing up on his computer. I started at the bottom of the tree, asking him if he had inserted the CD and run the installer. He hadn't. He had simply inserted the CD, which was immediately ejected. He hadn't installed the application. However, that was what he understood installation to mean. He was very upset, but he wasn't just some knucklehead. Most people I talked to were professionals and successful, but they weren't computer experts. It wasn't that they weren't intelligent; it was that we hadn't provided the proper toolkit. The instructions weren't clear enough.

So even though he was mad, and he spent at least thirty minutes on the phone to sort out the problem, there wasn't a feedback mechanism for me to raise my hand and let the company know that the onboarding bundles it was selling needed a few extra steps. Through that whole process, we were treated as the place where broken stuff had to be made right and not as a source of customer conversation to provide insights to make the product better. Moving forward, that mindset has to change.

When it comes to these two paths—social media and customer service—it's pretty obvious that today, social media is mostly used as a cheaper way to advertise, but it isn't being fully used to build real relationships. Social media should be used as a vehicle to deliver product information in a more cost-effective manner. It should be used to help validate why we're in business. These conversations may lead us to divest in a product, or even go out of business in order to defend our values. If companies don't have that level of conviction, they'll start to flounder over time.

Companies need to ask themselves if they are living their purpose just as you and I should get up in the morning and feel confident that we've done enough soul searching and had enough world experiences to understand what we want to stand for in life. Companies need to figure out what they want to stand for. If they do that effectively, they have a shot at finding product-market fit and realizing amazing commercial success. If they can't do that well, they should give the money back to the shareholders and go out of business.

Our personal insecurities sometimes prevent us from seeing and acknowledging that hard truth. It's popular for well-funded start-ups to pivot and change their core product and even target a different audience. Few companies pull that off. Most end up losing sight of their purpose, what they stand for, what customers they want to make happy, and as a result, they don't stay around very long.

Much of this is common sense, of course. But why doesn't every business follow this approach? One, there are certain industries that have not been forced to acknowledge that this is a world where the consumers' perspective, their sophistication, and their motivations have changed. Going back to the music industry, there were expensive trucks that needed to ship cassettes and CDs around, program directors at radio stations who had to be influenced to play new songs, and a limited number of music video stations like Viacom with MTV to promote on TV, which created scarcity. But over time, distribution channels got broader, promotional channels were more accessible, and production costs were reduced. When this happened, customers gained more control, more sophistication, and more insight, and the industry fell apart. There are other industries that haven't moved that quickly, but they will get there as well.

One of the reasons this isn't acknowledged as the new normal for all businesses is because there are certain industries that believe they can hold back these macrotrends. Your product may not be in the media or technology industry, but the reason I continue to use them as examples is because they are bellwether indicators for how other industries will be reshaped. The software industry exists in a highly accelerated innovation loop. The primary challenge the software industry faces is not technology related; it's human behavior related. These issues extend to a number of industries, but examples like the music industry are something of a canary in a coal mine.

There's a huge challenge in putting all of this into action. Almost everything mentioned in this book on how to actually solve this problem is hard. For starters, it's tough because in small companies, there are so many things that serve as distractions from focusing on the customer at a very deep level. Businesses believe that hiring a publicist or public relations firm and having articles written in *TechCrunch* or *Wired* are of the utmost importance. In probably any industry, a company wants to be discussed in its trades and publications. People believe those conversations will help them drive success.

Large companies, meanwhile, are obsessed with process and ways to standardize things, and the messiness of talking to small numbers of customers just doesn't make sense. Furthermore, if the company uses a handful of individuals to get really good at talking to customers, it becomes afraid those individuals will leave the company and take their customers with them. And while it's true that entrusting employees to maintain customer relationships comes with risks, it is even more risky to try to build customer relationships with people who never see real humans behind the corporate logo.

Most of this poor behavior is driven by misinformation or fear that doesn't lead to success. In the end, if you do it right, it's back to the fitness metaphor: if you want to get fit and you want to be your best physical self, you have to eat right and work out. And guess what? You can't do that just at the end of the year. You can't make it a temporary New Year's resolution.

You have to do that every day. You have to make it part of your lifestyle, and as a company, you have to build products where that's baked into all your processes rather than something that one department does or something the company rallies around for part of the year. It has to be sewn into the very fabric of the company.

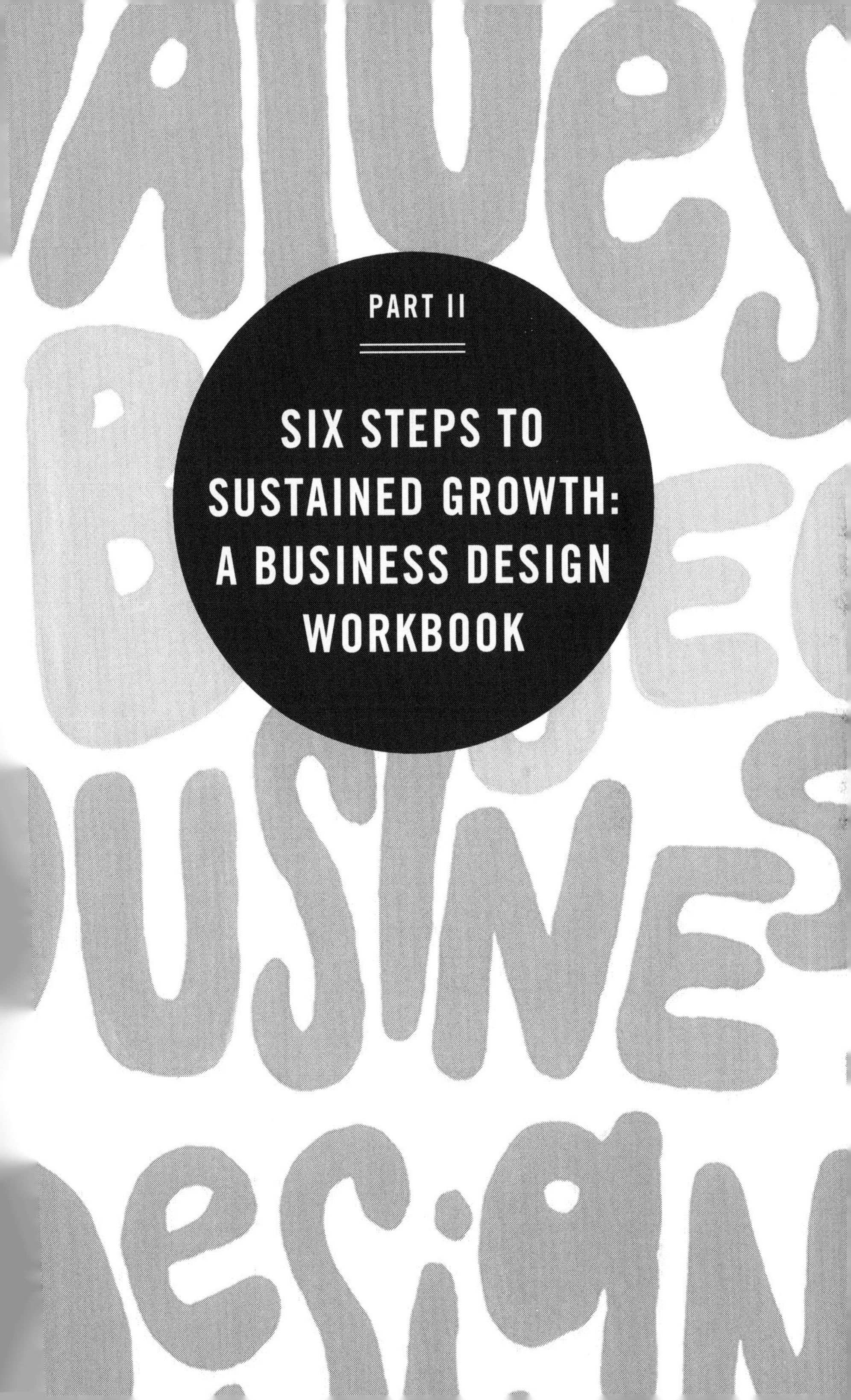

PART II

SIX STEPS TO SUSTAINED GROWTH: A BUSINESS DESIGN WORKBOOK

CHAPTER 4

STEP 1: ALIGN VALUES

IN THE LAST CHAPTER, I SHARED THE CORE SOLUTION OUTlined in this book, and to reiterate that message: listen to consumers and provide value every twenty-four hours. The first half of that—listening to the consumers—implies that you know which customers you need to listen to and what they care about. To do that well, you need to understand both what the customers care about and what the product, brand, or company stands for. In each case, this is about deeply understanding values.

The second half of that charter requires that you provide value every twenty-four hours. This is about frequently providing that value to the customers. It's important to distinguish between understanding customers' values as opposed to providing them with value. Values are what our customers and a company cares about. Value is what you trade with your customers. Once we understand the values that define both the customers and the company, you can determine how well you're aligned. The better the alignment, the better potential fit for a long-term customer relationship.

As you get to the execution stage, you have to figure out which tools are capable of doing this. I mean, that's a very obvious statement, but how do you actually put a process in place to track how well you're doing along the way? One of the available tools is called a values list exercise. At its most basic, this is a list of approximately sixty values. The goal is to choose the top six values for the individual or the company. There's nothing magical about a specific list, but when you force a decision-making process that prioritizes the top 10 percent, it allows you to see more clearly and filter out the extraneous. It ultimately unlocks a lot of underlying values.

In this book, I'll provide a sample list of sixty values (see p.147), such as *joyful*, *humor*, *family*, *love*, *adventure*, and so on. They're generally one- to two-word labels that infer something we truly cherish. Your goal as a company is to define yourself with values. Choose six, understanding that it doesn't mean that the other fifty-four don't matter but that you are making a conscientious choice to define yourself in a concise way, identifying the values that matter most to you.

My sample list should not be considered exhaustive, as it is only a template. If there are more precise terms that articulate your values, by all means, add them to the list. But at the end of the exercise, you should have exactly six values that represent your company. These are the values for which you would be willing to go out of business to defend. And if you're willing to commit to that, it's a very powerful statement. Often, a small company will begin to make products it didn't intend to as a reaction to the demands of the market; however, if those products don't align with your values, your customers won't know what you stand for, and it will be very difficult to stay in business anyway.

In a larger company, one of the challenges is getting all of your employees to stand behind your values so much so that they, too, are willing to defend them to the point of going out of business. The same with getting your shareholders to stand behind your values. And then, as I'll address more thoroughly later, you must ensure that your customers understand those values and your commitment to them. That's difficult but necessary.

Once you have built your own values profile, you need to do get a values profile of your current customers and the ones you seek to acquire in the future. But how? You aren't just going to send them a survey—or maybe you will. For some businesses, that strategy might be appropriate. Perhaps it's not the same list exercise that we've just discussed, but it might be something not too distantly related.

Short of directly asking customers in a survey, you could ask them how they spend their time, who the people are that they admire, and what types of activities they enjoy. From that, you should begin to deduce the sorts of values they likely have. In fact, there's often a substantive difference in the answers people give when asked a direct question in a survey, and how they behave in real life. The indirect route sometimes yields more accurate results. The key is to be empathic in observing both to what the customer says and what the customer does.

This can be very challenging for some product developers who might want to go directly to the customer to talk about the thing they're building without having taken the time to get to know that customer on a deeper level. The more time you invest in understanding your customers' underlying values, the more you'll be able to make wise decisions prioritizing the road map on the offerings that you provide.

Value alignment requires a strong conviction in the values you embrace. That said, you need to be flexible when your customers' values change. And their values will and do change, not drastically, as if they loved their family one day but not the next, but in subtle ways as they go through different stages in life.

A nineteen-year-old customer is not going to be the same a dozen years later because thirty-one-year-olds have a very different set of priorities. A person's responsibilities and perspectives change at each age, and it's incumbent on a company to embrace the evolution of its customers. The alternative—and the strategy that too many companies fall back on—is to allow those people to leave and opting to try to find new customers. As I've pointed out, the problem with that is that it's a very expensive proposition to court new customers.

A better strategy is to satisfy your existing customers by having them move through new lines of products and services. Relationship building is difficult and time intensive. To lose customers with whom you've developed a relationship is to squander all of that time and effort only to start from scratch with what are essentially strangers.

Once you've made that substantial investment into your customers, you have a good sense of what they stand for. That information will help you find those people when you want to share your message. How you broadcast that message is a topic for the next chapter. Bear in mind that it is very difficult to radically change one's brand values in today's world in light of the fact that once a person starts to observe a profile on a particular company or brand or product, it becomes set.

Ironically, it is actually easier for something that is perceived as a negative to be turned into a positive than the reverse. For instance, look at the perceived difference between George Clooney and Tiger Woods. Clooney, for many years, was *People* magazine's most eligible bachelor, dating around, with no sign of settling down. And while that might make good tabloid fodder, there's nothing newsworthy about it. He's single, he's successful, and this is the lifestyle he's chosen regardless of whether you personally agree with it or not.

Woods, by contrast, carefully crafted an image of a clean-living family man. He wrapped himself in family values and built his brand around them. So when the news broke about his secret adulterous lifestyle, controversy erupted and he was exposed as being hypocritical. His own values were not aligned with his brand's values.

When that happens to a brand, it becomes very hard to restore public trust. For Woods, the result was that many of his long-time sponsors pulled out because they couldn't be associated with his now-discovered values or the controversy surrounding him.

Situations like that, in which you let down your brand or company, raise a crucial point, and that is, don't commit to values that you don't believe and can't live up to. If you make a promise to be something and you fail to do so, you've lied to the public, and that's really hard to undo.

Your values are more than just words that you picked from a list because they sounded nice. It has to be your guiding set of principles, your raison d'être, and must be visible not only in your words but in your actions. Your values must be operationalized at every level, so deeply so that even your shareholders participate in living up to and defending those core beliefs.

CHAPTER 5

STEP 2: CREATE AWARENESS

NOW THAT WE'VE TAKEN A LOOK AT WHAT YOUR COMPANY stands for, and we understand what your customers or future customers stand for, and you've found alignment, you have to start telling them that you exist. You can't just stand there and expect folks to discover you. You have to create awareness so that they know not just that your product exists but that your values are driving that product.

Just as an aside, throughout this book, we talk about products and services, and yet we can usually interchange the words *product*, *service*, *brand*, or *company* because these rules apply so generally.

The first step in that process is being authentic in how you deliver your message. Authenticity is often confused with other concepts. Sometimes you'll see a brand—maybe it's an old, stodgy brand—that young adults do not find interesting, so it tries to advertise its message portraying itself as cool. Hot

Pockets hired Snoop Dogg to promote its product and had him alter his lyrics to substitute in the words *Hot Pockets*, as he pulled one out of the microwave. Then, he danced around with some kids. It just looked desperate.

In the brand's vain attempt to be cool, it came off as completely inauthentic. And that's a common problem because too many brands confuse cool with authenticity. Cool is a pillar that brands can rely on to reach certain audiences and share their values, but it only works if the spokesperson is someone who is confident enough to go against the grain. Coolness provides assurances for people who lack that confidence and gives them the imprimatur of someone who is respected for being a nonconformist.

Being authentic is really about just being yourself. And that doesn't matter if what you are is nerdy or boring or adventurous. Whatever qualities emerge from your values exercise, own them. Then, when you create awareness, be that. Present yourself in an authentic voice because that will resonate with your (potential) customers regardless of whether they care about the features of your product. Because there is a cacophony of inauthentic phonies out there, an authentic voice cuts through the noise and is heard crystal clear.

The list of values creates the tone and voice you'll use to speak to your customers and potential customers. Your values may not be the sexiest, but don't let that stop you. If you're in the insurance or banking industries, and your values are integrity and steadfastness, do you want Snoop Dogg rapping in your TV ad? Your audience has certain expectations that you will present yourself in a manner befitting the values you claim to hold, which, if you're properly aligned, are also theirs. Bach may not be as cool but is more in tune with your brand and your base.

Simultaneously, it's crucial to help people understand what makes your company different. Differentiation is really an important thing because it involves how people make sense of the world, and why they pick A over B. Once you've established the values that you share with your customers, look for descriptors that you think you can defend. And use objective words rather than subjective ones.

Great examples of objective differentiation are things like *only*, *first*, and *best*. I'd go as far as saying that is, in fact, the order in which you want to prioritize those. If you're trying to articulate how you're different, one way is to be the only company that does a certain thing. That's a powerful position. If you're not the only one, maybe you were the first. That resonates, too.

Again, avoid being subjective when you're trying to communicate what differentiates you. Everyone claims to be the best, but without standardized criteria, what does that even mean? You can claim to be the fastest, but then again, everyone claims that, using their own calculations. It's a bit like asking who is faster between a gold-medal sprinter and a gold-medal marathoner. The question is inherently flawed. And that's what weak brands rely on. Whether it's trying to sell you shampoo or an SUV, the ad will make claims that aren't objectively measurable.

The result of this murkiness is that the customer is unimpressed with your own accolades. It strikes the audience as self-congratulatory nonsense devoid of any practical value. It's like white noise or the fine print in a contract: it's unintelligible.

When you start creating awareness, you'll begin to get feedback. The next step is to do some research to determine if there are enough customers interested in the values that you've prioritized to make the business viable. You shouldn't be frightened away from your large aspirations, but be realistic about the challenges you might face if you're tackling a really small market or a market that's really hard to connect with. If what you stand for appears to be exclusionary, seek to find new ways to reach more customers. That might involve evolving your values to be more inclusive.

To recap: Be authentic. Explain how you're different. The next goal in creating awareness for your brand is to ensure that you land your message and communicate contextually. Contextual conversations are the way in which humans interact with one another, but it's generally not the way that companies communicate to consumers.

The traditional model is what's known as the interstitial ad, which you're no doubt familiar with. You're watching a program that you enjoy and it cuts to a commercial break in which an advertiser is hawking a product being pushed on you because you are part of the demographic that watches this channel at this time of day. It jumps out at you as an unwanted non sequitur. This form of advertising is turning from tolerable to completely irritating.

A better form of advertising involves participating in the conversation. This requires knowing where the audience is and what it cares about. And that ad should not be jarring or disruptive but, instead, should find a way to naturally insert itself into the conversation in an authentic manner. Increasingly, companies such as YouTube have realized they can't force everyone to sit through ads, so they have incorporated a Skip button, which becomes available a few seconds into the ad. If the ad hooks you, you can watch. If not, you're moving on.

And while that's a start, companies still haven't managed to perfectly match the advertiser with the market. If you're watching cat videos all day on YouTube, it would make sense that advertisers provide you with plenty of cat food commercials. What you shouldn't be plagued with is diaper and baby food ads. Maybe you actually do have a baby you should be caring for, but if so, there's a really good probability you aren't spending all day watching videos of cats.

The challenge is that creating good ads with quality production values is expensive. If you do spend a lot of money creating that ad, then you want everyone to see it. That costs money, too. The result is that, for the most part, only large brands have the pocketbook to make and run such ads. And even when they do, they run the risk of the public tiring of it. The more that it's seen, the more it loses its luster.

Audiences have short attention spans. There is a need for novelty. That's one reason that brands try so hard to create a series of ads that feature recurring characters or motifs. It's a way of continuing the story they're telling. They may even have a few. GEICO wants to flood the TV audience with its ads but knows that there are only so many celebrities from yesteryear that people can handle. Even though it has different personalities each month, it's still not enough GEICO. So the company uses the little green gecko with the Cockney accent, and once in a while, they'll even bring back the caveman, which did so well with audiences that they warranted several encores.

Because GEICO is heavily investing in advertising, the company can afford these ads that will carpet bomb viewers, who may or may not even need insurance. Meanwhile, the Italian restaurant in your own neighborhood, which you would like to learn more about before shelling out your hard-earned pay and hoping for a great meal, can't afford to advertise to you in such ways. It prints out fliers or a delivery menu and maybe offers a coupon to encourage you to try it.

The interstitial ad, lacking precision targeting, is merely an interruption in your customer's experience. It's a nuisance, which makes your brand a nuisance. There is a better way. Of course, it's still in the early stages, as evidenced by display ads that are seizing on a keyword you've typed into a search engine or a product that you recently purchased, but the idea is laser-focused relevancy.

One company that is making progress in this regard is Houzz. If you're in the market to do some interior design, remodeling, or just buy a few pieces of furniture, this website will provide a fantastic collection of photos available from just about any search term that you type in. The quality of the content is excellent, as is the quality of the tagging, which is a form of metadata. So the additional data attached to the photo are so well done that you actually get what you're looking for. Compare that with poor tagging in which you search for a banana but get photos of bandanas, or you are looking for a hoverboard but get skateboards, surfboards, and snowboards.

One area in which Houzz excels is in supplying additional data. If you're looking for a Grohe faucet, it will also give you the names and websites of a few companies in your particular area that will install it for you and a few DIY books on the subject. Introducing products and services in the context of the experience that the customer is in at that very moment is one of the best ways to demonstrate authenticity. That's the current state of the art in contextual communication. And we're getting closer to that.

Historically, brand advertising, or lifestyle advertising, has been a hard thing to quantify in terms of measuring consumers' responses. You just really didn't know what sort of effect your message was having except by looking at your numbers at the end of the month or quarter. Increasingly, that is changing. Sites like Pinterest are playing a large role in that.

Suppose you love to cook. You go to Pinterest and begin looking at different users' boards for ideas and inspiration. You find a blueberry salad that you want to make. You save the recipe, which calls for a particular brand of olive oil. You're savvy enough by now to know that this recipe is an advertisement in disguise from that olive oil company. But who really cares? That company found something you wanted and is helping you get it. Implicitly, it's acknowledging that it happens to be an ingredient in something larger than itself and showing you how it can show up in that context.

People just need examples sometimes. It's one of the reasons why furnished houses sell better than empty ones. "Staging" the house is just a way of providing the potential buyer some context as to what the house could be. The same is true of the olive oil. Nobody realizes its full potential as it sits in a bottle. But when it is shown living up to its potential, on that blueberry salad, the person seeing that "ad" has a much better understanding of what the product is and can be.

And again, this is an authentic way of communicating and showing up in a contextual fashion. The traditional method would involve interrupting *CSI* to tell viewers that their olive oil is better than the leading brand. This olive oil even differentiates itself in the fact that it brought you this recipe while the other brands merely intruded into your living room to interrupt your favorite TV program at a time when you weren't even remotely thinking about blueberry salad, much less olive oil.

CHAPTER 6

STEP 3: ACQUIRE CUSTOMERS

THE NEXT STEP IN THIS PROCESS IS TO GAIN CUSTOMERS. IF you know what you want, and you know what you stand for, then you need to let people know that you're out in the world. You don't just build it and hope they come; you must be proactive. Once you've completed the first two steps, you need to convert people into actual customers.

What you should be thinking about is the process that customers go through when they think about how and why they need your product. One of the traditional formulas used in this process is the value equation:

VALUE = BENEFITS – COST

Some product benefits are easy to calculate, while others are highly intangible. Nevertheless, we use different tricks in our brain to do this calculation when we buy. Product developers, companies, brands, and service providers are trying to trade value with their customers. In return for their product or service, they seek something else that customers value: time and money. They're trying to trade one form of value for another, and the process that customers go through in making that exchange is filled with decisions.

Much of customer acquisition is about helping current and future customers make confident decisions. If that is done well, those customers will come to a "yes" quickly when they want to consider buying your products, and they will have a stronger potential of being satisfied. Customers rely on rules of thumb when solving value equations. It's a heuristic method that factors in multiple variables.

Consider a person shopping for jeans. The price is $60. The customer weighs that cost against the benefits of the social status the jeans infer or the utility that they would provide. And perhaps that value seems right in line with that price point. The customer sees that as a fair deal. But suppose the price has been slashed from $120. Now, the perceived value of the jeans has doubled. The $60 price is now a bargain. But you can't just mark up your prices only to immediately discount them. Remember, the Internet gives customers better access to product information than ever before. You'll eventually be caught if you rely on tricks to deliver value.

Customers are constantly making decisions rooted in a discipline known as behavioral economics, which is the analysis of the financial decision-making process. If product developers are smart in how they help their customers make wiser decisions, they will make better relationships with their customers.

By learning how customers make decisions, you're able to understand their habits and patterns. One of those patterns is the customer's default choice. If you present a product as the best or most recommended, customers will generally be drawn to it. From there, you can add or remove components. A handmade bag, for example, can include extra straps or be stripped down to a bare-bones model, and the price can be adjusted accordingly.

With that in mind, if you offer a default choice for a product and provide a number of upgrade options, you can actually deter someone from buying the additions. If, instead, you offer a default choice with the option to remove features for a lower price, the perception is that it is a better deal. Where the original price may have been $500, removing the options makes it more affordable at $375, and the customer feels like it's a bargain.

There are all sorts of decisions you want to allow your customers to make in this process, but you want to refer back to their values list to understand how to do that in an empathetic way. You do not want to take advantage, nor do you want to exploit your customers during this process. Instead, you do want to respect the fact that they're using this process to make decisions. It will lead them to the cash register, and ultimately, you want them to make a purchase decision that they are happy with so they'll stay with you.

In all of this, there are a number of economic theories that have been developed over the years to articulate how decisions are made. Many models are flawed because they assume a world in which people consistently make rational decisions. The fact is, customers often behave irrationally. That's a hard concept to build a process around. However, if you have your values list and it's accurate, what may look like irrational behavior on the surface may actually be a very rational choice based on a prioritization of competing values.

There is a concept called prospect theory, influenced by the social sciences, among other fields. Experiments in this area have demonstrated that depending on how a choice is presented, people will make a decision very differently. According to a 1979 paper by Kahneman & Tversky, people don't make decisions in optimal ways, and they're willing to take on what seems to be an irrational risk depending on how their choices are showcased.

Here's the canonical example:

1. Which of these two options would you choose?

    - A 100-percent chance to receive $250
    - A 25-percent chance to win $1,000 and a 75-percent chance to win nothing

2. Which of these two options would you chose?

    - A 100-percent chance to lose $750
    - A 75-percent chance to lose $1,000 and a 25-percent chance to lose nothing

What this research showed is that when people are faced with a decision around a positive gain, they would opt for the lowest-risk alternative. In that context, they would take the guaranteed $250. But when they were given the second scenario in which it is perceived as more risky, they would choose the more risky option. They would rather choose risk in the negative scenario, not in the positive scenario.

The lesson here is that people dislike losses more than they like the equivalent gain. Keep this concept in mind as you walk your customers through the decision process because if you are writing advertising copy or presenting purchasing decisions in the absence of a real set of decisions that your customers face, they may choose what looks to you to be an irrational choice but is quite rational to them.

People tend to optimize for the present. When they think about value exchange, they typically optimize for a value exchange that is perceived to be front loaded, and they make decisions based on both time and the amount of information they have. There was a study done in the United Kingdom that asked a simple question: "Would people rather have £100 now or

£110 in a month?" It turned out that most people wanted the money immediately.

The key takeaway here is that behavioral change is driven by a lack of foresight to the future. When you anchor people in their future self and ask them how a decision will impact them when they're thirty or sixty, they start to optimize and make decisions that have a longer-term viewpoint.

Whether it's the time horizon of the decision or a certain social context, there are decisions people make with imperfect information where they have to make a selection simply using some rule of thumb or best practice. With small purchases, such as whether to buy a pack of gum, decisions are often made in a matter of split seconds, whereas with large purchases, there may be a lot of research involved to come to a decision.

If a customer is buying a new vehicle and is looking at an interior gallery of photos, the company doesn't know which of those photos the customer cares about. But if it understands the values of that potential customer, it will be able to filter out the photos from the original photoshoot that don't matter. As a practical way in which you can begin to apply this step, present choices that are going to be optimized for what you believe the attitudes and the values of the customer should be.

The core principle is this: if you help your customers make more confident decisions, you're able to increase the likelihood that they purchase your product. The customer-acquisition process is an attempt to introduce your products in the context of what you stand for, and then invite those customers to hang out with you so that you can exchange value.

Recall our metaphor of personal relationships being proxies for the relationship between customers and products. Once you've decided someone is the type of person you want to hang out with, you trade phone numbers (or maybe a Snapchat handle) and have light interaction. At some point, you need to have more than just coffee with that person for the relationship to grow. You have to spend time together to have a real relationship.

Eventually, you would invite that person to your house, but the first time you meet, it might be a more formal setting, such as a fancy restaurant. You're trying to provide a safe environment for both sides to get to know each other. After the first set of interactions, it's no longer a binary relationship. You start to understand more about what that person cares for and what he or she doesn't care for. The process becomes incremental in both our personal relationships as well as with our products. You can look at this as part of a spectrum.

When you're dating, you don't decide to go on a vacation together for the first date. You might get coffee first, then maybe lunch or dinner, and at some point, you might invite the other person over to your home for a barbecue. Then you would introduce that person to your friends, and in essence, you are expanding the relationship. The challenge for many companies is finding ways to achieve this without appearing to be cheesy. One of the first things to think about is where the customers spend their time, whom they spend it with, and what their activities are. How can you show up in that context?

If three women are having a girls' night out and they're catching up with one another, and a guy walks over and interrupts them, talking about a completely different topic, all three women won't just be indifferent, they'll be turned off. They may label him as the "weird guy" and avoid him the rest of the night. Any time they see him or any of his friends, they'll choose to walk away. That seems obvious, of course, but often, our brands are showing up in this manner. They're the weird guy in the club. It's a horrible way to start a new relationship, and it's not surprising that for many brands, they never get past that point of interaction. The weird guy may think he simply approached the wrong set of girls, so instead, he targets new ones. That mindset doesn't work.

It's fundamentally flawed because he's showing up out of context in an inauthentic way. He never gets past that first line, and worse still, he may be at the wrong place or there at the wrong time. It may not be the best place for him to show what he's about. If what he says he stands for is in conflict with the place he's in, his credibility is instantly shot.

This becomes a typical progression that companies need to embrace, and to do this properly, you need to find real opportunities to show up and in the proper context. Figure out where people go, whether it's a family event, hiking, community activities, or the like, and get out in the real world. The local businesses and community organizations in that area are always going to need a little support. It may not need cash support, but it may need something else of use. Provide your product in context in a smart way.

If you are a consumer packaged-goods company and you sell water, and there is a marathon or fun run for cancer, it's one thing to sponsor the jerseys, but it's another to give your water away. Handing out bottles of water allows people to experience your product in context. They're doing physical activity; they'll be thirsty and need a drink.

What's important in this case is asking yourself why you're there in the first place: it's because you care about cancer awareness. You are a brand that says you care about what these runners care about, so you're giving your product away for free. And even though most people are going to be savvy enough to realize this is a branding opportunity, it is nonetheless a much more authentic way to show up in the conversation.

For a technology company, buying an ad in a circular that advertises your software product as being 20 percent off may not be as effective as sponsoring free courses online that use the software. A college undergrad may be interested in learning music production and search for information on the web. It's more effective if that student sees free courses in music theory or music production that are sponsored by your company rather than the circular ad. Your company shows up in that conversation in a much more authentic way, and it's at a time when the customer needs you.

The last and most important aspect of the customer-acquisition process is to stop pretending that every day is a happy day. Everyone has fantastic days, and everyone has bad days. If you only show up on the good days and pretend the bad days don't exist, you can't expect to have a very deep relationship with someone.

To effectively acquire new customers, you need to show up when the customer needs you most, not necessarily when it's best for you to sell your product. The nuance here is that what they need from you, or what you might be able to provide, may not actually be what you sell. Or at least, it may not be what you exchange direct value for. If you want to get new customers, you need to find moments in their lives in which they need what you have to offer. And what you have to offer may not initially be the product you're actively selling them.

CHAPTER 7

STEP 4: BUILD RELATIONSHIPS

I'VE TALKED ABOUT ALIGNING VALUES AND ABOUT MAKING sure your future and current customers are aware of those values. I've talked about how to acquire those customers and get them to buy products at least for the first time. The next question is, "How do you keep those customers and continue to build that relationship?"

The next chapter will discuss engagement and retention, but in this chapter, I want to focus on making sure customers understand you'll be there for them. Simply put, it's about trust. Recall the definition of trust as the ability to predict future behavior.

Trust is not inherently a good thing. It is something that helps us predict how the world is going to behave, and how the people we have relationships with in the world will behave toward us. If you trust a criminal to be a criminal, you're not surprised when he or she behaves like a criminal. That does not mean the person you thought was a criminal is actually one. That's a dangerous perception you want to avoid.

On the flip side, if you trust someone to be friendly and caring and to be in your life for the right reasons, you have to attempt to be consistent around him or her. The Tiger Woods example highlights that because once you stop being predictable, it becomes hard for people to put their trust in you. For a company selling a product, once a customer loses trust, it's hard to build it back up. In some instances, you can never regain it.

What's interesting about Microsoft is that over the last few years, there has been a segment of the population saying that it was too aggressive in cutting certain products and didn't truly care about that customer segment. These customers didn't have a relationship with the brand and they felt the company didn't care. Microsoft acknowledged that perception and began to adapt, changing their actions and behaving differently. However, there's still a minority who refuse to listen to the new message. They have already decided that Microsoft cannot regain their trust.

On the path to building relationships with customers, you have to make sure you're investing in the relationship from the beginning and that you behave in a highly predictable manner. If that entails being less engaged in the beginning because it fits with how you want to engage over time, it may be the right decision for your company. If a new dating relationship begins with handwritten love letters and the sending of flowers, but two years in, those overtures completely stop, you're going to wonder what happened.

The past is a fair predictor of future behavior, and if you suddenly stop behaving in the same manner as before, you can rightly be called out. Making sure we behave in a way that is consistent is important, and that is coupled tightly with the company's values list. You have what you stand for, you have your values list, you've built customer relationships, but if you don't budget properly or if you cheat along the way, you won't be able to sustain that same level of service.

The challenge many companies have is that the payoff in the relationship may be further down the road. There is no short-term payoff. There is no profitability. It's hard to exchange value right away. This is a challenge for the high-growth products you're wanting to build. It's hard to build these relationships in an accelerated fashion and make them sustainable. It's the same reason a pop star can become popular very quickly and then disappear just as fast. What isn't rooted in a deep connection doesn't tend to last.

What makes this challenging for companies is the inability to predict the future outcome of the customer relationship. There is no guarantee that the time and money invested into a customer will lead to a transaction in six months. A smart approach is to spend time or other resources on what you have and on what you're willing to continue to give in perpetuity. If your cost structure cannot support this model, and you cannot keep giving your customer this service, it's not something you should consider as a relationship-building activity unless it comes with a direct monetary exchange.

This is a problem for companies large and small alike. On one hand, there are expectations from shareholders and investors to grow at a certain speed, but it's not always reasonable. You cannot predict when you will reach product-market fit, or the ability for the product to continually satisfy customer needs. You have to have enough reserves of creativity, time, money, and people to keep refining the process. You have to assess why you're setting those types of goals where you can't be successful. You cannot expect every customer interaction to be amazing.

Couples who have been married a long time will tell you there are great years in their marriage, but there were also years rife with struggles. There were things in life that they were either growing through or a challenge they faced, and it was hard. But the shared journey through thick and thin became valuable. That payoff is on both sides. When a couple in their eighties speak about their journey together, they don't just reminisce about the great times, they talk about the bad times, too. But the value they received by going through those bad times is that they shared in that journey together.

The takeaway from this is that while you're trying to build high-growth products, you can't assume that you can also accelerate the depth and value of the relationships you're building at the same velocity.

CHAPTER 8

STEP 5: ENGAGE AND RETAIN

THE PENULTIMATE STAGE IN THE RELATIONSHIP-BUILDING PROcess is to make sure that you don't just show up for the special events but that you're also there for your customers in both the good days and the bad. A big part of how you sustain the relationship is through engaging and retaining customers. How frequently do you need to interact with the customer for your business to be successful? You must find a way to maintain the conversation even when you're not transacting with the customers.

Engagement and retention is a key part of this. Quantitatively, retention is a measure of how many customers you keep in a given period. For certain businesses, that is tracked on a long time line. For others, it's measured on a very short one. In the auto business, loyalty for large purchases would be measured over many years, if not decades.

If someone owns a Toyota vehicle, for example, and a new version is coming out, that person will research months in advance to decide whether to trade up his or her model for a new one. Toyota, then, needs to begin spreading the message of what the new model can do and how it would benefit the customer early on. This requires buying ads and placing products in TV shows and films. It requires local events and campaigns or sponsoring a local community. These are all well-known techniques, but the challenge is that they're sporadic in their effectiveness. It can be proved that they do work, but there's no guarantee they will work. In addition, it requires a lot of capital to provide consistency with this type of approach, which is why brand-centered advertising campaigns are regulated for large national brands in the United States.

Technology has decreased the time cycle for when engagements can be measured, from long lead-times where someone may own a vehicle for years, to a cell phone owned for twenty-four months, all the way down to someone playing an app on their phone where the relationship for that is compressed. The result of that short relationship has created a dynamic in which certain companies, such as those in the software industry, have become very good at managing the user life cycle. As a result, they're good at measuring retention.

You can extrapolate the information you learn about user retention from companies that make mobile games and apps and apply it to other types of companies. For app companies, their user-retention rates are measured in days. They keep track of how many customers show up on day one and metrics that determine whether those customers remain the next day, for seven days, and for thirty days. Some companies use a twenty-eight-day retention metric to more closely map the weekly cycles. Nevertheless, we're able to group customers from the day they show up and become customers.

Suppose you create and launch an application, and on launch day, there are thirteen hundred new customers who download the application. That group of customers would be treated as a cohort and considered day 0 of the relationship. The next day would be day 1, and you would measure how many people who opened the app the previous day reopened. Then, you would measure again on day 7 and again on day 28.

This is a fairly unique opportunity because technology provides the ability to track all of these metrics passively using different web services, so there is no need to hire companies or marketing agencies to count or speak with these customers. It's counted in the background automatically and brings new insights so that you can run reports from all the data being collected.

No matter how good a product a company has developed, it will lose customers every day in almost every instance. There are very few businesses that gain a customer and then keep that customer in perpetuity. Instead of trying to aspire to zero customer loss, you need to be trying to keep your customers as long as you can. The reason retention is so important is that the effort it takes to establish those relationships is extremely high. The energy it takes to maintain those relationships in a healthy manner is much lower. As we've discussed, the cost to keep a customer in the software world is six to seven times lower than it is to acquire a new customer. With that in mind, it makes much more sense to keep your current customers happy than to actively pursue new ones.

When it comes to tracking cohorts, you can measure how many showed up on day 0, and then how many showed up on day 1. If the first day, 1,400 people showed up, and the next day there were 1,350, you can not only track the performance of a given cohort, but you can also track the performance against these groups. Knowing how your customers will behave as a group can help predict future behavior.

One thing that can be gleaned from these data is that not only do most services lose customers every day, but the earlier customers tend to perform better—both from a retention and monetization standpoint—than later customers. The common belief is that customers who show up later are less vested and more indifferent. It doesn't mean they don't care about the product, but they can take it or leave it. The insight you should take from this is that it's important to make sure the early-arriving customers continue to stay invested in the product. Keeping these customers happy is key because they will be the driving force of word of mouth and earned media. On the revenue side, they are also the most profitable customers.

A game title a colleague of mine worked on provides an example of this. The new game launched, and the customers who joined up in the first 60 days represented 30 percent of the entire revenue generated for that game over a period of two years. If the customers who showed up in the first 60 days had been neglected, they would have sacrificed almost a third of the revenue. This entire process of customer development is anchored in the idea of retention. While there is a fine resolution measurement of this in products such as software, where retention is measured in days, you can apply the same formulas to other businesses that need less frequent tracking, whether that measurement is a week or a month.

That said, this book is rooted in the process of building and sustaining high-growth products. One of the assertions here is that you can't do that if you don't have high retention and high engagement. There is nothing wrong with low retention numbers for a product, but it is highly unlikely that you can have low retention, low engagement, and simultaneously, high growth. If the premise of a product is that you want to build something that is high growth, or you want to sustain a high-growth product, the first piece of that puzzle is retention. The basic math here is similar to how the compound annual growth rate is measured in finance. The best financial investments grow exponentially through the compounding nature of reinvesting your gains. The same math works for growing and keeping a large customer base. The second piece of this puzzle is engagement. Engagement is a measurement of how much time you're spending with your customer.

When you think about the time in your day, there are main clusters or blocks of time. There is the time you're sleeping, the time you go to work or school, and then there is free time. If you look at a large technology company with access to all of its customer data, you can see how it tries to show up in the context of these twenty-four hours of your day. Companies like Samsung and Apple make devices that can be used throughout that twenty-four-hour period. Google tries to exploit the data and media you consume throughout that period. Microsoft and others like it do a great job figuring out how to make you more productive during your work period. Then there's the king of engagement and retention: Facebook.

Facebook does a fantastic job of looking at the section of your life that you would consider free time. In today's world, that's not necessarily a fixed, continuous block of time. You may look at your phone during the middle of a break or while commuting on the bus, but nevertheless, the aggregate of those three to six hours you have in a given day. Mark Zuckerberg and the product teams at Facebook are masters of nabbing as much of that time as they can.

If you have experiences that lead to high engagement, you can do interesting things to maintain that customer relationship. It's one reason that Facebook has done so well and serves as an example of what we should think about concerning the gold standard of engagement and retention. Facebook has the ability to build a product that you want to use every day, and that increases its value as you continue to use it. And because your content is now in this service and more difficult to get out, it creates a virtuous loop. That, in turn, creates a network effect, where the service becomes more valuable as more of your friends and coworkers use it. Facebook hits the trifecta of the necessary components of high engagement and retention.

That's a powerful concept, and without it, you can end up in a strange place with your customer relationship. If you think about your friends as a metaphor, there are certain friends you see frequently and others you only see once in a while. That doesn't mean the friends you see every day are your most important friends, but you have a different relationship with those two types of individuals. As you're building products, you should be explicit in how you work with or how you build relationships, the time you expect to spend with the customer, and how often you expect them to have interactions. People who want to make a product that has low engagement or retention is fine, but they should not expect to turn that product into a high-growth product with a large customer base without investing vast amounts of money to build that relationship.

To actually go out and put this idea into action requires a value proposition. It must speak to the user's values, making sure the core action in the experience is something that resonates with the customer. This requires measurements that you can't estimate. The one-day, seven-day, and twenty-eight-day retention figures represent one type of measurement, but to the extent that you can use technology to track data, you should measure everything. How many times did a customer use a loyalty card? How many times did someone call the lobby downstairs? There are any number of activities that can be tracked with regard to a customer relationship. For a given business, there should be a mapping that shows which actions map to which part of the relationship life cycle. Measurement is important regardless of how it's done, as long as the data are accurate.

Once you have the capability to measure activities, you need to be able to test changes in the product or the way in which you market the product's capabilities. One approach is through A/B testing, where you test two or more options for a new experience on a small subset of your total audience. Let's say you have a software service with a million customers who come every month. They would be called monthly active users. You want to increase the retention of those monthly active users, and you want to see if you can do a better job in getting the message out about new features in an attempt to see if it helps retention.

So out of, say, one million customers, one thousand customers would be selected, and you would put them in control group A. Then, take another thousand customers and put them in control group B. You do not tell customers they are in a control group. For group A, you continue doing business as usual, as you always have. For group B, you may add a small pop-up in an ad that lets them know about three new features that maybe weren't highly discoverable. The experiment could run a day, a week, or a month to suit your needs.

For websites, it's easier to run A/B tests than it is for an app in which there may need to be updates for the application or game. But regardless at the end of the experiment, you would look at the data and as expected see that control group A had no change in their retention. Then, you can look at control group B to see if they had a material impact or a lift in retention—meaning you kept more customers during that period when showing that particular piece of content. If that happens, you can have higher confidence that the pop-up in that instance is something that will build higher retention.

Once you have ended the experiment and run the analysis, you can decide to roll out that capability or feature to the entire population of one million users. This concept of continually running A/B tests is critical not only with regard to how you track retention, but also how you optimize it over time.

In-experience messaging is a key tactic used frequently to send messages to customers. If you walk into a store and there are items in the back you didn't know about, or if you launch an app and there are new features you didn't notice, you can't discover the new capabilities. Even with something simple like using Spotify, there might be a great album you can't discover if you don't know where to look. The ability to expose the user to other parts of the value proposition—whether in the real world or digital—is important to increase the perceived relationship value with that customer.

Another tactic used is the onboarding experience for new customers. If a customer walks into a store for the first time and browses the aisles, at some point, an employee should approach her to ask how she can be helped. Upscale retail stores typically do a good job of helping you find what you need. If you go into a store like Barneys, the first thing employees will do is attempt to get your name and information because they have a database of almost every customer who has walked into the store. They know how much and what type of items you buy. They know what stores you visit in different cities. When you show up to the store, they will start to build a profile on you to determine your needs and wants. They have highly trained personnel who are memorizing all these data and logging them into the system later.

The initial experience of Barneys onboarding makes you feel that they care and gives you insight into what the relationship could be over time. As a result, they are able to sell people $2,500 slippers. Obviously, they're targeting the upper side of the consumer market, but the reason they're able to sustain this is because they look at the relationship holistically, and they make sure when you first show up that they're doing the right things. They have your information from the beginning and now have a direct line of communication to update you on new products.

That direct line of communication is important for sustaining a good customer relationship. As mentioned previously, record labels did not have the information as to who was buying their music. They couldn't communicate with the customer even by proxy. Regardless of the industry, if someone is managing a customer relationship, the business must have a strong commitment to own at least one communication channel for the relationships it is building with customers. One of the popular channels is digital because it helps track communications over time. That can be called a push message. You want the ability to push messages to the customers who have opted in.

You want to use that as a point to both engage and reengage your customers in a way that will drive retention. This happens frequently with customer relationship management e-mail systems, where a customer will receive an e-mail stating why a new product has been created and how it can be used. The e-mail shows up unprompted and is a way to pull the customer back into the experience.

Text messages can be used, or if a company has a mobile app, it can use push notifications. These are ways to let the customer know you are thinking of them while also telling them about something they may be interested in.

Some companies fail at this despite doing a decent job of maintaining the push notification channels because their copy doesn't read right. So every e-mail received by a customer contains copy such as, "Biggest Sale Ever! 70% off!" This isn't a conversation starter. What would be better is something more akin to "Summer is right around the corner," and the company knows the customer is going to take a trip or that he or she likes to swim. They put the product in the context of those values and planned activities. Those are the companies that do a good job at leveraging push messages.

Even small businesses can take advantage of these messages. With today's scheduled services, there are a number of software services that are inexpensive. For as little as $20 a month, a local restaurant can sign up for a service in which every receipt has a call to action such as, "Text or e-mail us and tell us how we did." This can also be used for loyalty points or similar programs. Once you use that active point of engagement to capture contact information, you can follow up. Rather than having a marketing person in the back of the restaurant poring over hundreds or thousands of customer records, you can automate each time customers visit and log their e-mail address and phone number.

There are also background processes that can notify you if a customer hasn't showed up in the last sixty days, and it can automatically send him or her a canned e-mail or coupon as a text message. That way, it doesn't matter if customer A is in a different stage than customer B. The clock ticks, and if the customer hasn't shown up in a given period, it can send a message. That's called marketing funnels or e-mail funnels, and it is a way to pull the customer back into the conversation and build more authentic relationships. Those are actionable steps to dig in and deliver on the promise and the compounding potential of improving engagement and retention.

CHAPTER 9

STEP 6: REINVEST

THE FINAL STEP IN THIS PROCESS IS TO REINVEST. BY THIS point, you've learned to understand your product's values and how to align them with your customers' values. You have created awareness that your product has been launched into the world and that you've developed relationships with the customers whom you've acquired. You've taken those relationships and sustained engagement and retention, which has culminated in monetizing and generating income for the value you've been providing. This is a hard process, but if you have the discipline and rigor to put them into place, you'll be successful. Now it's time to take that success and refine your product to meet your customers' evolving demands.

There will still be the future equivalent to an "as seen on TV" infomercial, where products like Snuggie and ShamWow have been sold in great quantities. These types of products won't sustain, and they won't be high growth. What you need to do through this entire process is to take a breath and then start the whole process all over again. No matter how great a job you do, your customers are going to leave. It may be because they're in a different stage in life or it's just not feasible anymore for them to use your product. It's not that your company or your customer did anything wrong; that's just a part of the cycle. You will need to start relationship building all over again with a new cohort of customers in order to replace the ones you've lost.

This is a continuous process that requires a lot of discipline to not only understand where the product is in this flow but also where your customers are in terms of their life cycle with the product. The world in which you made a product, packed it into a box, put it on a truck, delivered it, and then someone paid you for it has been totally disrupted.

In a way, that process was much like the way that movies were made. Studios would assemble a team of multidisciplinary talents who were each experts in their fields, and they'd set off on a mission to tell a great story. For a given time, maybe six months or a year, they would put together a film. They wouldn't tell their customers exactly what they were making. There would be a trailer and the stars would do interviews for the press, but the product was essentially a surprise. There was no Rotten Tomatoes in the old days, nor was there the Internet, for that matter.

When the film was at last released, most of the investment needed to be made back in six to eight weeks. Sometimes the product launch would go great, but other times it would go horribly wrong. As a result, studios needed large holding companies that could stay afloat funding these films so that the hits could sustain the duds.

Back in 2012, Disney tried to launch a new franchise called *John Carter*. It reportedly spent $250 million producing the film and $100 million marketing it. Disney dropped the ball on marketing. Customers didn't show up. Disney reportedly lost $200 million. Part of the reason was because the film wasn't that good, of course, but a lot of lousy movies still turn profits. The real problem was that the movie was marketed incorrectly.

These days, your product must be good for it to be a success. You can no longer coast mediocre products past your customers. In this case, the *John Carter* trailer did a really poor job showing what the experience was. When you start to drive up awareness, you need to be smart about how you introduce and position your product. Disney didn't understand the customer it was targeting. It attempted to market *John Carter* as having broad appeal, a so-called four-quadrant film, but it didn't resonate with a strong base because most consumers were indifferent. Disney had no base of values in the film, so it didn't have a group of customers to connect with. In the end, the film flopped, and Disney had to go back to the drawing board.

The people in the film industry who make the films, whether we're talking about independent films or blockbusters, take several months off after production is complete if the film has been successful. That might be when they're seen in tabloids taking a vacation and seemingly living the good life. If during that time the movie did well, they could go back and negotiate a new project. They get back together with the same group of people, or sometimes a brand-new group, or they start all over again.

That method worked in a world where there weren't many choices for the customer. If there are only a handful of movies premiering, you could choose from one of those based on genre. If you wanted to see an action movie, that's what you chose. People were grouped together in a bloc. Now, when Friday rolls around, there are more movie choices in theaters. There are movies on Netflix. There are other activities that can be done that don't involve a movie at all. The idea of just showing up without continually talking to your customers is really hard to do anymore.

Increasingly, creating service-oriented products is less and less like the movie-making process. Instead, it more closely resembles a nightly newscast or talk show. It's a different organizational muscle because there is no hiding in the corner from everyone. You have to show up every day at a certain time because the news simply has to run. From the top of the hour until you wrap, everyone has to be on their job.

For his talk show, Jimmy Fallon has to have a new monologue every night. He may take a vacation, in which case, they rerun a few episodes; but most nights, a new show has to run. The news runs nightly; there's no such thing as a rerun. In the old days, you could make a product, and if you got a hit, you could sit back and let the money flow in. The world simply doesn't work like that anymore.

People who still want that type of business shouldn't try to build high-growth products. Consumers are not broadly willing to pay $18 dollars for a Blu-ray movie that they've never seen. In fact, they're increasingly not willing to pay to "own" something they have already seen and even enjoyed because they can likely stream it whenever they want or buy a digital version for much, much less.

The Internet has driven transparency to the point that consumer behavior has shifted. The products you make today are increasingly service oriented, and you have to show up every day or you're going to lose your customers. If you have poor retention, every metric of your business goes down. From large, multinational conglomerates to small businesses, certain company cultures have gravitated toward specific business success metrics. Certain teams talk about their sales growth, while others talk about quality. Even with a four-star Amazon product, which is worth tracking, if you still have poor customer retention, you won't win.

As you think about how to reinvest in your customers, you have to remain laser focused on retention throughout the process. As you start back at step one, you need to take all of the information you've learned on this journey and work that into other stages to do a better job of retaining the new customers who show up to your business.

CONCLUSION

A FEW YEARS AGO, A FRIEND OF MINE IN COMMERCIAL REAL estate development asked me to come with him on a trip to Cuba. He was looking at opportunities to develop real estate there in the future, and figured with my technology background, some ideas might spark as I observed the country. Perhaps I would even find a way to bring my ideas to Cuba. It turned out that I learned a lot more about myself and about America going on that trip than anything else. The realization that something was different was immediate. Upon landing in Cuba, one of the first things I noticed was that there is no advertising.

As we drove down the street, there were no billboards. The market had no ad or sales paper. There was no competition among cereal brands. There was messaging on the packaging itself, but there were no sales advertisements to entice you to buy the product. Even on TV, there were no commercials. We watched a televised baseball game, and during the break between innings, instead of commercials, the camera panned around the field. I had a heightened sense of awareness about the lack of advertising from the beginning of my visit.

At the same time, I noticed that people generally seemed happy. Now, this doesn't mean Cuba is an ideal place to live. As an American, we're afforded many things and we're very fortunate. That said, the people were genuinely happy. Children were playing stickball in the street and seemed perfectly content with what they were doing.

When I observed this, I started to wonder if the lack of advertising correlated to the perceived contentedness of the people. When I began looking at data sets about inequalities in different environments, one of the things I found was that when you have the expectation that the person next to you has the same deal as you, you remain content with your own. The kids in Cuba did not know what they didn't have, and there was less disappointment or reason to be disappointed. Now, if some had iPads and some didn't, that would be a different story. That would be a very American story.

Another thing I noticed was that there was less crime. Cuba is not far from Florida, but if you visit metropolitan Miami, the crime rate is high. There is a huge economic disparity between the haves and the have-nots. There are Ferraris and Lamborghinis racing down South Beach; there are yachts and beachfront estates. Simultaneously, there are hungry children and out-of-work parents in the same area.

Those who lack economic opportunity are naturally going to be discontent. Reasonable people will see that most of those people earned those fancy things, and that will be a good incentive to work harder. A certain percentage of people, however, will see those things and want to simply take them for themselves. This friction spawns the idea that the world is not fair. This lack of perceived fairness drives much of the dialogue in America today. We all have our different values, but most of us believe a system should show up that gives each of us a fair shot at achieving what we want.

As I look at the scenario in Cuba and I've pored over countless data, the rise of advertising has paved a wave of discontentedness that manifests itself in unhappiness. This is a terrible thing because we've allowed creatives from brands to reset our expectations on what we deserve, and as a result, we feel like we don't have what we need in life. One of the reasons I'm such as strong advocate of technology is because it holds the promise of making the world more equitable and fair. We should be able to work hard and be successful, but the playing field should be level. Information shouldn't be held back, and products shouldn't be represented as being great when they aren't.

With the two-party political system in America, both left and right deal with the issue of having a representative who might be a terrible option. However, there is so much distrust in government leadership that we as a collective American people are willing to elect the wrong people just to challenge a broken political system full of inequality. The key here is that public officials haven't recognized or acknowledged that the population has moved away en masse from the old way of thinking into a world where citizens can make the best decision if given all the information. When that happens, true democracy can be cultivated. Part of that is showing up in your customer's life journey in a meaningful way. In this example, the customer is the American citizen. The problem with many of today's politicians is that they are focused on exploiting customer values rather than embracing them. Government is being run like music labs in the 1990s.

When you ask people who are in their seventies or older, rich or poor, what mattered most in their life, there are two things that resonate: the relationships they had and the memories they created along the way. You are foolish if you don't take that perspective and factor it into the way in which you show up in your customers' lives. It's not just your relationship with the customer but also how you facilitate the other relationships in the world.

Facebook used to get laughed at because people didn't get it. They didn't understand why someone would post about being at a restaurant. What Facebook did was to create a software platform that helps manage relationships when someone is not next to you, and increasingly, we are building relationships with people who aren't next to us. Memories are the moments in which you reflect on the ups and downs of your journey. When you look at those on Instagram and Snapchat, what they are doing is creating artifacts, almost like an index card at a library, to trigger a memory contained within. It works the same way as a pop song might trigger a memory of a prom dance or a wedding.

Those are triggers to emotional hooks that are attached to memories. There's a reason photo start-ups in the software world have been so popular. Pictures are a cheap way to produce an index card to trigger memories. You do yourself a disservice if you're not building products that ultimately map to these meaningful things in someone's life journey, his or her relationships, and his or her memories.

We can take this further and say that we're trending toward a world where people broadly have sort of an allergic reaction to solely focusing on materialism. People want to make things; they want to be unique. It isn't that people no longer want nice things, but there's an evolution in which people are more desiring of experiences than material things. People are willing to pay not just for the right to say they own something but also for the right to have an experience that creates new relationships and new memories.

For companies, the challenge is that these are hard to mass produce. Many companies need to grow on a large scale, but they don't have the systems to deliver these experiences, which their customers value the most.

The value equations for goods, like for the price of jeans, for example, is easier to evaluate than an equation for experiences.

When considering that value equals benefits minus cost, it's easy to plug in numbers for a pair of jeans and then consider how durable and well-made they are before deciding what additional social capital is received from wearing that brand. Because customers have access to better information, they can spot a deal on hard products much more easily, which means it's harder to extract high margin out of them. A TV sold at Best Buy or Amazon may only have a 5-percent margin because consumers are highly aware of what it costs to manufacture the television, and the margin gets squeezed out. On the other hand, it's difficult for someone to run the same value-equation analysis on an experience. As a result, there's much more profit margin to be had if you can deliver an amazing experience.

This trend of consumers' growing preferences toward experiences is important, and companies need to embrace the idea of being service oriented. Even if a company doesn't see itself as a service company today, it needs to think of how it can show up in that context.

In the fast fashion world, companies like H&M and Forever 21 are finding the cheapest ways to make fashionable clothing. High-end fashion may be able to sell clothes at higher price points, but they aren't able to mass produce or grow to a larger scale because the customer base at those prices is a niche market. Forever 21 found a way to make a top for $1.50, which includes outsourcing production in another country for $0.50, and then spending marketing dollars to get the top to retail for $12.

The goal of these fast-fashion companies is to have a recurring revenue stream in which customers return often. Their foundation is predicated on a false premise because they are trying to condition people that if they don't want to be seen in the same outfit as someone else, they should return to buy new items every Thursday. It creates a buying loop. Consumers are now more aware of this action, so they're starting to spend their dollars in places where they feel the relationship is more honest and where they're not being peddled into new products just for the sake of the money they bring to the table.

Almost every product catering to younger customers will need a social bottom line. TOMS shoes for example, has an interesting business model with its one-for-one philosophy. For every pair of shoes sold at retail, a pair will be donated to a country in need. That may not make sense for every business, but each industry should look to embrace authenticity in this manner. You get that authenticity by understanding who you are and what you stand for, and that starts with the values the company believes in. You need to deeply understand the values that you're willing to defend at all costs and find ways to live those values every day.

People and brands labeled as being "cool" are the ones that knew what they stood for, and even if it was unpopular, they stayed the course. In a world where many of us are trying to figure out what we stand for, when we see that confidence in someone else, we see that conviction; it gives us a North Star to position ourselves to be like them. When people see someone who's authentic, they want to wear the same types of clothes, use the words they use, and follow in their footsteps. This isn't just for kids; this applies to businesspeople as well. They see what other successful businesspeople are wearing and decide they need the same suit to signal their own success.

Whatever you stand for, being authentic has to be key. Once you have that, go find the customers who share the same values. As you come together, build that relationship. The companies that truly embrace this, rather than just using it as a marketing message, are companies that will be successful. Even if the goal is purely quantitative and someone wants to make a product to generate the most revenue, aligning values and being able to articulate those values with the customer is the best way to get predictable revenue streams. When life inevitably gets rough for a brand, those are the customers who will stick with you.

At the end of this journey, if you're successful, it will have been hard. It will feel like a lot of work, and you will wish for an easier way to make a dollar. But the result will be a better set of relationships and a better bank account—and ultimately, products you'll be proud to have made.

VALUES EXPLORATION

Here is a list of values you can use to explore what is most fundamentally important to your product, brand or company. You can also use this as an individual exercise. This list isn't meant to be comprehensive and you should feel free to add your own values to the list. The purpose is to identify values that define why your product, brand or company exists. To complete this exercise, you pick six values. Your list of six doesn't need to be sorted in any order, but ***you can't select more than six***. Have fun.

Accuracy
Achievement
Advancement
Adventure
Autonomy
Balance
Beauty
Belonging
Challenge
Clarity
Commitment
Communication
Competition
Cooperation
Creativity
Critical
Curiosity
Civility
Diversity
Duty
Effectiveness
Equality
Excellence
Excitement
Face
Family
Forgiveness
Freedom
Fun
Growth
Harmony
Health
Helping Others
Honesty
Honor
Humor
Independence
Innovation
Integrity
Justice
Kindness
Knowledge
Leisure
Love
Mystery
Peace
Power
Prestige
Productivity
Quality
Reciprocity
Relationship
Religion
Respect
Risk
Security
Self-Realization
Service
Solitude
Spirituality
Strength
Structure
Teamwork
Time
Tranquility
Uniqueness
Unity
Variety
Vitality
Wealth
Winning
Wisdom

ABOUT THE AUTHOR

LASEAN IS A SEASONED TECHNOLOGY EXECUTIVE WHO HAS worked on some of the largest consumer technology products in the world. He began his career in the US Navy, built his software engineering and user experience skills at early-stage startups, and helped pioneer entertainment services on mobile phones. He's also founded multiple companies and worked as a consultant for clients that include Cablevision, Electronic Arts, Sony, T-Mobile, Target, TOMS Shoes and Warner Brothers Studios.

He currently manages the Windows Experiences business design team at Microsoft and helps build products across form factors that include AR/VR, game consoles, mobile and PC. He's been fortunate to help launch products that have found their way into the hands of millions of people. His quest continues to fill the world with fresh ideas, new sounds, bold images, and captivating experiences.

Made in the USA
San Bernardino, CA
01 February 2017